# DEBORAH

## BECOMING A WOMAN
## OF INFLUENCE

A Bible study based
on the teaching of

———

NANCY DeMOSS
WOLGEMUTH

© 2021 *Revive Our Hearts*
First printing, 2021

Published by *Revive Our Hearts*
P.O. Box 2000, Niles, MI 49120

ISBN: 9781934718803

Printed in the United States of America.

Adapted from the teaching of Nancy DeMoss Wolgemuth by Erin Davis, Micayla Brickner, Laura Elliott, and Mindy Kroesche.

As you work through this study, use this space to doodle, color, and meditate on God's Word and consider how the story of Deborah gives you true hope.

———

FOR WHATEVER WAS WRITTEN IN FORMER DAYS WAS WRITTEN FOR OUR INSTRUCTION THAT THROUGH endurance & THROUGH THE encouragement OF THE Scriptures WE MIGHT HAVE hope. ROMANS 15:4

## DEBORAH AND BARAK

[1] And the people of Israel again did what was evil in the sight of the LORD after Ehud died. [2] And the LORD sold them into the hand of Jabin king of Canaan, who reigned in Hazor. The commander of his army was Sisera, who lived in Harosheth-hagoyim. [3] Then the people of Israel cried out to the LORD for help, for he had 900 chariots of iron and he oppressed the people of Israel cruelly for twenty years.

[4] Now Deborah, a prophetess, the wife of Lappidoth, was judging Israel at that time. [5] She used to sit under the palm of Deborah between Ramah and Bethel in the hill country of Ephraim, and the people of Israel came up to her for judgment. [6] She sent and summoned Barak the son of Abinoam from Kedesh-naphtali and said to him, "Has not the LORD, the God of Israel, commanded you, 'Go, gather your men at Mount Tabor, taking 10,000 from the people of Naphtali and the people of Zebulun. [7] And I will draw out Sisera, the general of Jabin's army, to meet you by the river Kishon with his chariots and his troops, and I will give him into your hand'?" [8] Barak said to her, "If you will go with me, I will go, but if you will not go with me, I will not go." [9] And she said, "I will surely go with you. Nevertheless, the road on which you are going will not lead to your glory, for the LORD will sell Sisera into the

hand of a woman." Then Deborah arose and went with Barak to Kedesh. ¹⁰ And Barak called out Zebulun and Naphtali to Kedesh. And 10,000 men went up at his heels, and Deborah went up with him.

¹¹ Now Heber the Kenite had separated from the Kenites, the descendants of Hobab the father-in-law of Moses, and had pitched his tent as far away as the oak in Zaanannim, which is near Kedesh.

¹² When Sisera was told that Barak the son of Abinoam had gone up to Mount Tabor, ¹³ Sisera called out all his chariots, 900 chariots of iron, and all the men who were with him, from Harosheth-hagoyim to the river Kishon. ¹⁴ And Deborah said to Barak, "Up! For this is the day in which the LORD has given Sisera into your hand. Does not the LORD go out before you?" So Barak went down from Mount Tabor with 10,000 men following him. ¹⁵ And the LORD routed Sisera and all his chariots and all his army before Barak by the edge of the sword. And Sisera got down from his chariot and fled away on foot. ¹⁶ And Barak pursued the chariots and the army to Harosheth-hagoyim, and all the army of Sisera fell by the edge of the sword; not a man was left.

¹⁷ But Sisera fled away on foot to the tent of Jael, the wife of Heber the Kenite, for there was peace between Jabin the king of Hazor and the house of Heber the Kenite. ¹⁸ And Jael came out to meet Sisera and said to him, "Turn aside, my Lord; turn aside to me; do not be afraid." So he turned aside to her into the tent, and she covered him with a rug. ¹⁹ And he said to her, "Please give me a little water to drink, for I am thirsty." So she opened a skin of milk and gave him a drink and covered him. ²⁰ And he said to her, "Stand at the opening of the tent, and if any man comes and asks you, 'Is anyone here?' say, 'No.'" ²¹ But Jael the wife of Heber took a tent peg, and took a hammer in her hand. Then she went softly to him and drove the peg into his temple until it went down into the ground while he was lying fast asleep from weariness. So he died. ²² And behold, as Barak was pursuing Sisera, Jael went out to meet him and said to him, "Come, and I will show you the man whom you are seeking." So he went in to her tent, and there lay Sisera dead, with the tent peg in his temple.

²³ So on that day God subdued Jabin the king of Canaan before the people of Israel. ²⁴ And the hand of the people of Israel pressed harder and harder against Jabin the king of Canaan, until they destroyed Jabin king of Canaan.

Caught up in a detrimental cycle of sin, the Israelites were the epitome of broken people living in a broken world. But God, who longs to see His people live in faith, surrender, and holiness, is willing to fight for the hearts of His people.

Enter: Deborah. She was a woman appointed by God as a judge—a woman used by God in a significant way in her day. As you watch this story unfold, you'll see how it all points to a loving God who faithfully carries out His promises and calls His people back to Himself. He turns weakness into strength and fear into faith for the good of His people, and ultimately, for His glory.

Though an unexpected candidate to be chosen for such a calling, Deborah courageously stepped out in faith as an instrument of God's deliverance. We'll see her life as a picture of how we can embrace God's beautiful design for us as courageous, godly women.

### WHAT YOU CAN EXPECT TO LEARN

Expect these five themes to embed themselves in your heart through this study:

- **Trust the Promises.** Deborah believed the Word of the Lord. We'll learn how to stand on God's promises and trust Him to lead and enable us.
- **Embrace God's Design.** Through Deborah's example, we'll discover how to embrace the beauty of God's design for our identity as women.
- **Trust and Obey.** We'll see the danger of disobeying God and the magnitude of His grace. Deborah, Barak, and others will show us how to respond to the Lord in obedience despite our hesitations.
- **Surrender to His Purpose.** When God places a calling on our lives, He equips us to fulfill His purposes. We'll see how He uses us as instruments for His glory to share the truth of the gospel.

- **Become a Woman of Influence.** As we see Deborah's demonstration of humble valor, we'll learn how to become women who exert a godly influence on others through Christ who lives in us.

TIPS FOR USING THIS STUDY

As you use this study, ask yourself:

- What does this passage teach me about the heart, ways, and character of God?
- Is there an example to follow or avoid? If so, how should I seek to change in response?
- How does this passage point to Jesus and the gospel?

Each week of the study is divided into five suggested daily lessons, but feel free to work at your own pace. Do what works for you!

You may also find it beneficial to listen to the audio series "Deborah: A True Woman Joins the Battle" at ReviveOurHearts.com/Deborah.

Remember, the Holy Spirit helps us understand God's Word. He is a gift and a "Helper" who is able to "teach you all things and bring to your remembrance all" that the Lord has said to us (see John 14:26).

Secondary tools to help you better understand the Word of God (but aren't necessary) include:

- An English dictionary to look up the basic meaning of words
- Various translations of the Bible (a good online tool is BibleGateway.com)
- A concordance
- A Bible dictionary
- Commentaries
- A study Bible
- Colored pens or pencils to write in your Bible

We've included group discussion questions at the end of this book. Join the conversation about Deborah with the *Women of the Bible* podcast created to accompany this study. Find it at ReviveOurHearts.com/WomenoftheBible.

Throughout the next six weeks, the *Revive Our Hearts* Team hopes you:

- Find practical wisdom to apply to your daily life.
- Read your Bible with greater passion.
- Delight in the Lord's design for your identity.
- Step out in faith where the Lord is calling you.
- Let Jesus use you as an instrument for the gospel.
- Know God better as a result of this study.

## *Israel During the Time of Deborah*

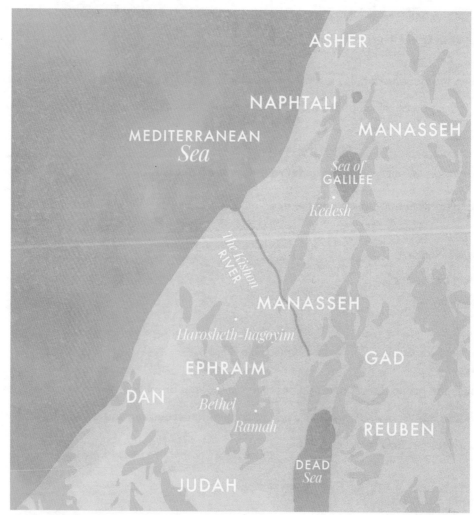

Spend time meditating on and memorizing the following verse this week:

then the LORD RAISED UP judges, who SAVED them out of the hand of those who plundered them

JUDGES 2:16

## AUTHOR

The Bible does not say
who wrote Judges, but
most scholars agree that it
was written by the prophet
Samuel. Samuel was the
last of the judges (Acts
13:20).

## WHEN

Judges is both a book of the
Bible and a historical period.
The period of the judges
began after the death of
Joshua (Judg. 2:6–10). The
judges ruled Israel for about
300 years (approximately
1380 BC to 1050 BC). [1]

## WHERE

The book of Judges takes place
in Israel following the Israelites'
conquest of the Promised Land
(Judg. 2:6). The book opens
with the death of Joshua in
a time of relative obedience
for God's people. The book
concludes with Israel in moral
and spiritual decline when
"everyone did what was right
in his own eyes" (21:25).

# Week 1

FROM DISOBEDIENCE TO DELIVERANCE

*Big Idea:* OUR DISOBEDIENCE
AND DISTRESS LEAD TO GOD'S
DISCIPLINE AND DELIVERANCE.

Wash. Rinse. Repeat.

Plant. Water. Harvest.

New moon. Waxing crescent. Full moon. Waning crescent.

So much of our lives operate in cycles. The book of Judges
describes a cycle God's people lived in for nearly 300 years:
disobedience, discipline, desperation, deliverance—the Four Ds.

Even though they had:

* experienced God's care during their wilderness wandering
* successfully marched into the land He promised them
* witnessed the consequences of rebellion many times
  before

...the Israelites put themselves in the spin cycle of
disobedience over and over (and over!) again.

And over and over (and over!) again, God raised up deliverers—
the judges—to call His children back to Him.

> Then the LORD raised up judges, who saved them
> out of the hand of those who plundered them.
> (Judg. 2:16)

The book of Judges lists twelve judges, handpicked by God as deliverers, including Deborah, a woman of faith and fortitude—*a true woman who exerted strong, godly influence in a distinctly feminine way.*

The cycle of the Four Ds didn't end with the period of the judges. As broken people living in a broken world, we all gravitate toward this cycle. As you dig into the book of Judges this week, may God's Word point you to Jesus, *your* righteous Judge, and remind you that He is able to fully deliver you from the cycle of sin and shame.

# Day 1: *The Danger of Disobedience*

*Read Judges 1–2.*

Every parent knows children don't have to be taught to disobey. Two-year-olds throw tantrums without a lesson on how to do so. Kindergartners sneak sweet treats, even when their mothers warn them not to. Teenagers don't rebel because they're teenagers; they rebel because they're human.

Write out your definition of disobedience.

_____

_____

_____

Though we may be tempted to think that rebelliousness, disobedience, and defiance are reserved for those who don't acknowledge God's authority in their lives, God's Word tells us differently.

## THE END OF AN ERA

The author of Judges wrote two introductions to this Old Testament book. Judges 1 and Judges 2 both begin with the death of Joshua, who succeeded Moses as the leader of God's people (Josh. 1:1–9).

According to Exodus 7:7, how old was Moses when he stepped up to lead the Israelites out of slavery in Egypt? _____

According to Deuteronomy 34:7, how old was Moses when he died? _____

Though Scripture does not provide as many details about the timeline of Joshua's leadership, Bible scholars believe that he led the Israelites into the Promised Land around 1406 BC and died at age 110 (Judg. 2:8) around 1380 BC, meaning Joshua ruled approximately how many years?

_____

Moses' total years of leadership   **+**   Joshua's approximate years of leadership   **=**   Years of godly leadership

Strong, godly leadership did not result in perfect obedience among God's people. The Old Testament records many times when the Israelites disobeyed God's Law during the period that Moses and Joshua led the nation. Still, Joshua's death marked a pivot point toward ongoing and worsening disobedience.

According to Judges 2:10, what defined the generation born after Joshua's death?

_____

_____

What was the result (v. 11)?

_____

_____

_____

A lack of godly leadership combined with the Israelites' failure to focus on God's character kicked off a vicious cycle, ushering in the period of the judges.

Read the following:

• Judges 2:11
• Judges 3:7
• Judges 10:6
• Judges 13:1

What did God's people do over and over?

_____

*Read Judges 2:12–13.* How did the Israelites rebel specifically?

_____

_____

These were the people of Israel—God's chosen, covenant people—bowing at the altars of pagan gods. We tend to focus on the sins of unbelievers, but the book of Judges sends a strong message: **God is concerned about the holiness of *His* people.**

Look up the following passages. In a word or two, write down the theme of each passage.

LEVITICUS 19:2

1 PETER 1:15–16

1 THESSALONIANS 4:7

Can you think of examples from Scripture where God called His children to turn away from idolatry and toward pure worship of Him alone? Write down whatever comes to mind.

_____

_____

_____

*Revisit Judges 2:11.* Write out the verse below.

_____

_____

_____

Like the Israelites, the tendency of every human heart is toward idolatry, the worship of something or someone other than the one true God. This is always an act of disobedience, worthy of divine discipline.

Ask the Lord to use this study to grow your commitment to turn from worshiping anything except Him. Write a prayer expressing your desire to be holy as He is holy.

Lord,

_____

_____

_____

Amen.

# Day 2: *Be Strong and Courageous*

*Read Judges 2:14–15.*

Think back to a time when you experienced appropriate discipline from a parent or teacher. How did you feel at the time?

_____

_____

The book of Judges shows us that human disobedience always leads to divine discipline. In the moment, discipline is always painful.

*Revisit Judges 2:14–15 below.* Circle all of the words that describe the discipline received by the Israelites as a result of their idolatry.

> So the anger of the LORD was kindled against Israel, and he gave them over to plunderers, who plundered them. And he sold them into the hand of their surrounding enemies, so that they could no longer withstand their enemies. Whenever they marched out, the hand of the LORD was against them for harm, as the LORD had warned, and as the LORD had sworn to them. And they were in terrible distress.

Based on your experience with discipline, do you think God's children recognized their distressing circumstances as God's correction? Why or why not?

_____

_____

Israel's idolatry wasn't a one-time mistake. Over and over they disobeyed God's commands; over and over they experienced divine discipline. Why do you think the Israelites didn't turn from their sin once and for all?

_____

_____

Why don't we turn from our sin once and for all?

_____

_____

Judges 4 finds the nation of Israel facing another leadership vacuum. How did they respond (v. 1)?

_____

_____

Again, God responded with discipline. Write out Judges 4:2 below.

_____

_____

This time, divine discipline came in the form of a Canaanite king. What is the significance of Jabin being a Canaanite according to Genesis 17:8?

_____

_____

Jabin was an enemy inhabitant of the land that God had gifted to the Israelites. When God promised to bring His people back to the land, He specifically commanded them to drive out the Canaanites (Deut. 7:1–6), but He never asked them to do it alone. He vowed to send an angel before them as they systematically drove their enemy from the land. Surely a command straight from God accompanied by an angelic warrior would inspire God's people to obey—except, of course, it didn't.

*Read Judges 1:27–36.* In your Bible, underline every time the Israelites disobeyed God's command to drive out their enemies.

The description of God's discipline continues in Judges 5:6–8. Circle the specifics of His chastisement below.

"In the days of Shamgar, son of Anath,
     in the days of Jael, the highways were abandoned,
     and travelers kept to the byways.
The villagers ceased in Israel;
     they ceased to be until I arose;
     I, Deborah, arose as a mother in Israel.
When new gods were chosen,
     then war was in the gates.
Was shield or spear to be seen
     among forty thousand in Israel?"

Beneath the chastening hand of God the Israelites were forced to live under the oppressive rule of the Canaanites, enemies from whom God had promised deliverance if only they had obeyed Him fully. They were outnumbered and overwhelmed: afraid, discouraged, and "in terrible distress" (2:15).

Have you experienced the Lord's discipline? If so, what did He use to expose your rebellion?

_____

_____

_____

_____

_____

Think back to that moment of human discipline you described at the beginning of today's study. How do you feel about that moment now? Has hindsight changed your perspective?

_____

_____

_____

_____

The Bible provides rich hope concerning the Lord's discipline. What beautiful truths do the following verses teach?

PSALM 94:12

PROVERBS 3:12

HEBREWS 12:6

Most of us can look back at the discipline we received as children and realize it was rooted in love and for our good. God's Word gives us the perspective that divine discipline, though painful, is a gift grounded in love. To wrap up today's study, write out a prayer thanking the Lord for loving correction in your life.

_____

_____

_____

_____

_____

# Day 3: *A Turning Point*

*Read Judges 4:1–3.*

Twenty years.

That's long enough to finish your entire primary education and start college . . . long enough to get married, have children, and build a life . . . long enough to watch your child grow from toddler, to teenager, to twentysomething . . .

And it's a long time to experience the Lord's discipline.

*Revisit Judges 4:3.* Underline the phrase that indicates how long the Israelites lived under the oppressive rule of Jabin and his general, Sisera.

> Then the people of Israel cried out to the LORD for help, for he had 900 chariots of iron and he oppressed the people of Israel cruelly for twenty years.

It took intense discipline over two decades to get the Israelites' attention. Why do you think they resisted the Lord's correction for so long?

_____

_____

_____

_____

Look up the following passages then use the word cloud on the next page to circle words and phrases that Scripture uses to describe **people of Israel.**

DEUTERONOMY 9:6

DEUTERONOMY 31:27

EXODUS 32:9

NUMBERS 14:27

stubborn

arrogant

cooperative

rebellious

stiff-necked clever

COMPLIANT

submissive cheerful

Look up the following passages then use the word cloud below to circle words and phrases that Scripture uses to describe **God.**

EXODUS 34:6

DEUTERONOMY 4:31

ROMANS 2:4-5

happy tolerant gracious

forbearing harsh

slow to anger kind

MERCIFUL

abounding in patient

love & faithfulness

Stubborn rebellion is human nature; longsuffering and mercy is divine nature. Through the lens of God's character, we see that His discipline is not intended to squash us but rather to humble us, to bring us to the end of ourselves so that we recognize our need and turn to Him.

Describe a season of stubborn rebellion in your life or in the life of someone you love.

_____

_____

_____

Consider Laura's story. Like the nation of Israel, Laura experienced the Four Ds.

**First, she disobeyed God's command by breaking her marriage vows (Heb. 13:4).**

*Last September I attended my first True Women Conference.*[2] *I didn't want to go, because I did not look forward to the correction I anticipated enduring. You see, I was two years into an affair. While I knew it was wrong, I did not have the resolve to walk away.*

*The first night's session was like the music and message had been chosen specifically for my heart. When we had a chance to anonymously submit a prayer request, I figured that was my only chance to truly have a shot at ending my cycle of sin. So, I turned in my card that night, went through the remainder of the conference, and went home to resume life as "normal."*

**Then, she encountered the Lord's discipline . . .**

*My life continued to spiral out of control for the next ten months.*

**Which led to desperation.**

*I reached a point of despair that I didn't know existed, and I confided in two friends. In that moment, I tasted the beginning of a forgiveness and freedom that I thought had slipped through my fingers.*

**Ultimately, Laura experienced the Lord's deliverance in a dramatic way.**

*Unbeknownst to me, it was also only the beginning of another painful journey. One of the friends I confided in was also involved in an affair—with the same man. In the midst of the hurt, our friendship has been strengthened, and both of us can see the perfection in the timing.*

*I know beyond a shadow of a doubt that this is answered prayer. I made a foolish decision based on my flesh, and I have consequences for it. But I am also reminded in an extremely real and tangible way that God is bigger. Bigger than my mess. Bigger than my hurt. Bigger than my sin.*

*I have been given a tremendous wake-up call and opportunity to pour into my marriage and family. God did not let me lose them, and that is a massive mercy.*

It took Laura two years to become desperate enough to respond to the Lord's discipline with a desperation to change. It took the Israelites two decades, but eventually what did they do? (Judg. 4:3).

Disobedience $\rightarrow$ Divine Discipline $\rightarrow$ _____

King David knew this pattern well. Second Samuel 11 records David's affair with Bathsheba, the wife of another man. As a result, David experienced divine discipline and eventually cried out to the Lord in desperation. David's desperate prayer for deliverance is preserved in the Bible as Psalm 51. Write out verses 1–4 in your own words to conclude today's study.

_____

_____

_____

_____

_____

# Day 4: *Deborah: God's Instrument of Deliverance*

*Read Judges 4:4–7.*

Think about the many ways we use versions of the word "instrument":

- Musical *instruments* make up the sound of an orchestra.
- Surgical *instruments* fill hospital supply rooms.
- A pilot flying without the help of autopilot flies *by the instruments.*
- A team member who plays an important part in a successful project is *instrumental.*

Here are a few other nouns frequently used in definitions of "instrument."

- Tool
- Implement
- Apparatus
- Means
- Device
- Document

And then this one— *"a person used by another as a means to some private end."*[3]

The instrument itself is a functional yet passive force. Every instrument works at the will of its operator. Keep this in mind as we continue to look at Deborah, who served as God's instrument to fulfill His good purposes.

*Read Judges 2:16.* Who did God use as instruments of deliverance for His people?

_____

_____

_____

_____

Look up the verses below and record the name of each judge.

INSTRUMENT #1: JUDGES 3:7-11 _____ Judged for forty years.

INSTRUMENT #2: JUDGES 3:12-30 _____ Judged for eighty years.

INSTRUMENT #3: JUDGES 3:31 _____ Judged for unknown number of years.

INSTRUMENT #4: JUDGES 4:4 _____ Judged with Barak for forty years.

INSTRUMENT #5: JUDGES 6:11 _____ Judged for forty years.

INSTRUMENT #6: JUDGES 10:1-2 _____ Judged for twenty-three years.

INSTRUMENT #7: JUDGES 10:3-5 _____ Judged for twenty-two years.

INSTRUMENT #8: JUDGES 11:1 _____ Judged for six years.

INSTRUMENT #9: JUDGES 12:8-10 _____ Judged for seven years.

INSTRUMENT #10: JUDGES 12:11-12 _____ Judged for ten years.

INSTRUMENT #11: JUDGES 12:13-15 _____ Judged for eight years.

INSTRUMENT #12: JUDGES 13:24-25 _____ Judged for twenty years.

As you review that list, jot down anything that stands out to you about Deborah specifically.

_____

_____

List the three things we learn about Deborah from Judges 4:4.

1.

2.

3.

The next verse tells us that Deborah would sit underneath a palm tree—apparently one that was named after her—between Ramah and Bethel in the hill country of Ephraim. Turn to the map on page 8 and draw Deborah's palm tree.

Now circle Harosheth-hagoyim, where Captain Sisera lived. This was the epicenter of the action as the tribes battled the Canaanite armies. Notice that it's about sixty miles to the northwest of where Deborah would have lived.

*Read Judges 4:4–10.*

Now review Judges 2:16. In the United States, cabinet members serve "at the pleasure of the President." At whose pleasure did Deborah serve?

_____

_____

_____

As a rule, those God raised up to provide leadership for His people—whether priests, prophets, judges, or kings—were men. Yet the people of Israel sought out Deborah to provide wise judgment for their daily lives. What types of qualities must she have possessed, humanly speaking, that would have drawn God's people to look to her for wisdom and discernment?

_____

_____

_____

Who did Deborah summon to execute God's plan to deliver His people from the hand of the Canaanites, and where was he from (Judg. 4:6)?

_____

Look at the map. Is that closer or farther from the action?

*Read Judges 4:6–7.* Write down the prophetic message Deborah gave Barak.

_____

_____

_____

_____

According to Deborah, who gave the command for Israel to "Go"?

_____

_____

What part of verse 7 might give Barak pause in going forward?

_____

_____

_____

_____

But what guarantee did God give to Barak about the battle and the outcome?

_____

_____

_____

_____

Deborah was an unexpected instrument of God's deliverance. She was a woman. Her home was far from where the action was. Yet God chose to use her. The unexpected mercy of God is that **He uses whomever He wants, however He wants, to accomplish His purposes.** God's choice of Deborah as an instrument of deliverance not only saved His people in her day but provided a model for us to surrender our lives as instruments in God's hands.

To conclude today's study, draw a picture that represents your desire to be an instrument used by God's hand.

# Day 5: *Take It Home; Make It Personal*

If you've sat in many traditional worship services, you've probably sung the famous lyrics from the beloved hymn, "Come, Thou Fount of Every Blessing."

*Prone to wander, Lord, I feel it; prone to leave the God I love.*

God's people have always been prone to wander. We see it in the Israelites who lived in Deborah's day, and all too often we see it in our own lives.

**Circle the word "again" in the passages below.**

*And the people of Israel again did what was evil in the sight of the LORD.* (JUDGES 3:12)

*And the people of Israel again did what was evil in the sight of the LORD.* (JUDGES 4:1)

*The people of Israel again did what was evil in the sight of the LORD and served the Baals and the Ashtaroth.* (JUDGES 10:6)

*And the people of Israel again did what was evil in the sight of the LORD, so the LORD gave them into the hand of the Philistines for forty years.* (JUDGES 13:1)

To help you remember what you've learned, write down the steps of the Four D cycle in the chart below.

Prayerfully reflect on your own life. Using the chart below, write in the margins about a specific time you kicked off the Four D cycle by choosing to disobey God and then experienced divine discipline, desperation, and ultimately deliverance.

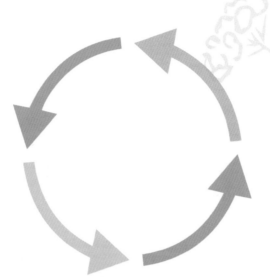

We could look at those charts and feel defeated by our repeated tendencies to sin, or we could look at them and feel grateful for God's repeated gift of grace. **The book of Judges is a book about Israel's rebellion, but more importantly the book of Judges is a book about God's deliverance.**

As you reflect on your own life, is there a pattern of sin from which you feel you cannot break free?

_____

_____

_____

_____

_____

_____

_____

_____

When we sin and say, *I can't believe I did that again,* God's Word reminds us that those moments are what grace is for. Grace woos our hearts and draws us back when we've been drawn toward idols. Grace interrupts the Four D cycle in our lives. Grace sanctifies and sustains us; it helps us to persevere in our faith. *Because of God's grace, the cross of Christ takes care of the again and again (and again!).*

To wrap up this week's study, write out a prayer of gratitude thanking God for the cycle of His grace in your life.

_____

_____

_____

_____

_____

_____

_____

Spend time meditating on and memorizing the following verse this week:

Charm is DECEITFUL & beauty is VAIN, BUT A woman who FEARS the LORD IS TO BE praised.

PROVERBS 31:30

# Week 2

*Big Idea:* DEBORAH EXERTED STRONG, GODLY INFLUENCE IN A DISTINCTLY FEMININE WAY.

For as long as artists have been painting, *mothers have been a source of inspiration.*

French painter William-Adolphe Bouguereau turned to oil and canvas to depict Mary sweetly holding baby Jesus on one hip and a lamb on the other in *L'Innocence.* Famous Renaissance painter Raphael famously depicted Jesus' relationship with His mother in *The Madonna of the Chair.* The painting hangs in a gallery in Florence and shows baby Jesus with chubby arms and legs, nestled cheek to cheek with His blessed mama.

Tour the Metropolitan Museum of Art and you'll find *First Steps, after Millet,* an oil and canvas work Vincent van Gogh painted to celebrate the birth of his nephew. The masterpiece shows a mother gently holding the outstretched fingers of her toddler as the baby takes his first steps. Remarkably, even early cave art unearthed by archeologists reveals images of mothers carved into stone walls.

As is often the case, art imitates life: *haven't we all been inspired by the nurturing power of mothers?*

In Judges 5, Deborah paints a self-portrait with her words.

> "I, Deborah, arose as a mother in Israel." (v. 7)

She didn't see herself first and foremost as a ruler, a judge, a prophet, a leader, or an influencer, though all of those descriptors would have been fitting—*Deborah called herself a mother.* It was as a mother that she inspired God's people to victory.

As you get to know Deborah more in your study this week, may you be inspired by the world-changing power of a mother's heart.

# Day 1: *Meet the Cast*

*Read Judges 4–5.*

While this study is focused on Deborah, we'll meet many other people in the pages of the book of Judges. Deborah, Barak, Jabin, Sisera, and Jael all play significant parts in Israel's deliverance and many others filled supporting roles. Ultimately, however, this story—*every story in Scripture*—is about God.

Using Scripture, give a brief description of each individual.

JABIN (4:2)

DEBORAH (4:4-5)

BARAK (4:6)

SISERA (4:2, 7)

JAEL (4:11, 17, 21)

To better understand the dynamics of the story, write down the names of the characters that fall into each of the following categories.

| ISRAELITE | CANAANITE |
|-----------|-----------|
|           |           |

| MALE | FEMALE |
|------|--------|
|      |        |

| MILITARY LEADER | CIVILIAN |
|-----------------|----------|
|                 |          |

Based on what you know about these individuals so far, who is the hero of this story?

_____

_____

_____

Which characters might be the villain(s)?

_____

_____

_____

We don't just open our Bibles to read about people who lived a long time ago. We open our Bibles to read about the character of God, who is alive and at work right now. Every person in God's Word was created to point to Someone bigger—Jesus. Every story in God's Word points to the bigger story—the gospel story.

We'll get to know this cast of characters over the course of this study, especially Deborah, a woman of valor. Using the word cloud below, circle words that describe someone who embodies valor.

*noble* fearful
cowardly timid
*determined* heroic
F E A R F U L
unwilling *bold*

Deborah's life inspires believers of every era. Her story encourages us to embrace God's plan for our lives with courage and boldness. Her example reminds us that women can be a powerful force for good. But ultimately, Deborah's story points us to the Director of every story, God our Deliverer.

Write out a prayer asking God to use this study to give you a bigger picture of Himself as you study His Word.

_____

_____

_____

_____

Make a list of the "cast" in your own life. Next to each name, write out a prayer asking God to use your story to point them to Him.

| CAST MEMBER | PRAYER |
| --- | --- |
| | |

| CAST MEMBER | PRAYER |
| --- | --- |

# Day 2: *A Righteous Judge*

*Read Judges 2:16–23.*

When you think of the word "judge," what comes to your mind? Write or draw your answer.

*Read Judges 4:4 below.* Circle the two words that describe Deborah's role among the people of Israel.

> Now Deborah, a prophetess, the wife of Lappidoth, was judging Israel at that time.

Prophet and judge are among the specific roles that God instituted for His people. Look up the passages below and write a brief description of each.

JUDGE

**Judges 2:16**

_____

_____

_____

_____

1 Samuel 8:4-22

Deuteronomy 17:15

_____

_____

_____

_____

Leviticus 21:6-8

Numbers 3:1-10

_____

_____

_____

_____

Deuteronomy 18:18-19

_____

_____

_____

_____

Much as they are in our modern judicial system, judges were appointed to oversee the application of law—God's Law—in the lives of God's people. Kings were intended to give righteous leadership and to build a nation focused on fearing God. Priests made offerings to atone for the sins of the people and in response to God's holiness were to live in a way that was set apart. Prophets spoke God's words to God's people as a means to call them back to pure worship.

How do these definitions add depth to your understanding of Deborah's roles as a "prophetess" and "judge"? What was she responsible for? What was she not responsible for?

_____

_____

_____

_____

Write out Judges 2:16 and 18 below.

JUDGES 2:16

_____

_____

_____

JUDGES 2:18

_____

_____

_____

Go back and circle who raised up each judge. Draw a box around who was with each judge.

*The judges were not self-appointed.* They were not chosen in an election by popular vote. Each judge, including Deborah, was handpicked and established by God. This lays an important foundation for our understanding of Deborah's story. To help this idea stick, fill in the word "God" in each of the blanks below.

Deborah was appointed by _____.

She spoke words given to her by _____.

She was used as a deliverer of the people of _____.

God's fingerprints are all over Deborah's story. More accurately, God used Deborah to play a role in *His story.*

*Revisit Judges 4:5.* Based on your understanding of God's intent for judges, what kinds of disputes do you think Deborah heard and resolved from her "bench" under the Palm of Deborah?

_____

_____

_____

_____

_____

Though Deborah was appointed by God to play a specific role for a specific time, each of us has been created to bear God's image (Gen. 1:27) and to give Him glory. Look up the following passages about God, our Judge. Next to each one jot notes about what kind of judge God is.

PSALM 7:11

DANIEL 4:37

ISAIAH 30:18

ROMANS 11:33

To wrap up today's study consider, has there ever been a time when God selected you for a specific role in a specific season? Write about it below.

_____

_____

_____

_____

# Day 3: *A Mother's Heart*

*Read Judges 5:6–7.*

Describe three roles you fill using the space below.

_____

_____

_____

Did you describe yourself as a mother? How about a daughter, grandmother, or friend? Though there are many cultural messages announcing that men and women are identical and interchangeable, God's Word declares: *we're different in some vital ways!* These differences are so important that they show up in the way we define ourselves.[1]

Social researchers have found that a man's sense of self is often defined through achievement and accomplishment. In contrast, women tend to define themselves by the quality of their relationships. Fulfillment comes through supporting friends and family and building thriving connections.

*Revisit Judges 5:6–7.*

In your own words, describe the cultural climate of Deborah's day.

_____

_____

_____

_____

How did Deborah describe herself?

_____

_____

Why do you think Deborah defined herself this way?

_____

_____

_____

It's interesting that Deborah didn't identify herself as a prophetess, a judge, or a leader. God used her in those roles, but that's not ultimately how she described herself. Beyond the circumstantial role of bearing or adopting children, what defines mothers? Make a list below.

_____

_____

_____

_____

_____

Mothers nurture. They care. They protect. With the heart of a mother, moved with compassion by the distress of God's people, Deborah got involved. _Scripture doesn't tell us if she had physical children of her own (though it it seems likely that she did), but it is clear that she operated from the distinctly feminine identity of motherhood._

Few forces of nature are as formidable as a mother bear who perceives that her cubs are in danger, thus the phrase "mama bear." Mothers of every species, including humans, are prone to rise up boldly when they feel that those in their care are in danger.

Have you ever seen or experienced "mama bear" instincts? Write about it below.

_____

_____

_____

What do you think might have caused Deborah's mama bear instincts to kick in on behalf of Israel?

_____

_____

_____

Look up the following verses. Write a summary beside each reference.

EXODUS 20:12

PSALM 127:3-4

PSALM 113:9

PROVERBS 31:27-28

What do these passages teach us about God's heart toward motherhood?

_____

_____

_____

_____

A woman can be a tremendous force for good. **When we have a heart to shepherd with compassion, we are in a position where God can work within us and speak through us. As He did with Deborah, God can use us to influence many generations.**

Can you think of other mothers in Scripture who wielded influence through compassion and care? Make a list.

_____

_____

_____

_____

_____

Have you ever heard a woman say, "I'm just a mom"? Perhaps you've said those words yourself. In our achievement-driven world, motherhood can sometimes feel like a lesser calling, but viewing motherhood through the lens of Deborah flips the paradigm back to the truth we find in Scripture. Deborah wasn't "just a mother." She was _just_ a judge. She was _just_ a prophetess. She was _just_ a leader. In her own eyes, motherhood was primary; everything else was secondary.

Are you a "mother in Israel"? Do you care about what is happening to the children in this generation? Is your heart grieved by what is happening to our families? Do you feel deep compassion for the hurting in our world? One way to respond is through intercession. There is something special about a mother's heart that cries out in prayer, saying, "Lord, we need You! Help us! Direct us. Show us what to do."

To conclude today's study, write out a prayer of intercession from your heart.

_____

_____

_____

_____

# Day 4: *Tough or Tender?* [2]

*Read Judges 4:6–10.*

"It's a Boy!" or "It's a Girl!" is usually the first fact announced at the birth of a baby. Some people claim sex ought to be of no consequence to a person's identity or role. But author Elisabeth Elliot disagreed. She published a compilation of notes to her daughter on the meaning of womanhood, in a book called *Let Me Be a Woman*. Reflecting on the meaning of femaleness, Elisabeth wrote to her daughter:

> Yours is the body of a woman. What does it signify? Is there invisible meaning in its visible signs—the softness, the smoothness, the lighter bone and muscle structure, the breasts, the womb? Are they utterly unrelated to what you yourself are? Isn't your identity intimately bound up with these material forms? [3]

What do you think Elisabeth was trying to tell her daughter?

_____

_____

_____

If you were trying to describe what it means to be a woman to a girl you love, perhaps your daughter or granddaughter, what words would you use? Make a list.

- _____

- _____

- _____

- _____

- _____

- _____

- _____

Elisabeth Elliot wanted her daughter to understand that the differences in a woman's body testify to the fact that God created her to have a different role than a man. She wanted her to take note of the "invisible meaning" of the visible signs.

Male and female differences are profound. A man's body is structured in such a way that he is the one who moves out and toward and has strength to give. A woman's body is structured in such a way that she is the one who welcomes, draws in, and has capacity to receive and nurture.

When the Lord presented the first man with his wife, the man burst out into a poem that expressed this fundamental difference. Read Genesis 2:23 below. Circle the word "Woman" and "Man."

> Then the man said,
> "This at last is bone of my bones
>     and flesh of my flesh;
> she shall be called Woman,
>     because she was taken out of Man."

In Hebrew, the name with which the male identified himself was *ish*, while his name for a woman was *ishshah*. This appears to be a clever and profound play on words. The sound of these two Hebrew words is nearly identical—*ishshah* merely adds a feminine ending—but the two words have a complementary meaning. Many scholars believe that *ish* comes from the root meaning "strength," while *ishshah* comes from the root meaning "soft."

Fill in the blanks with the corresponding meaning:

Woman = Hebrew *ishshah* = _____

Man = Hebrew *ish* = _____

What do you think the term "soft" implies about who God created women to be?

_____

_____

_____

## Do We Still Have Prophets?

In the book of Deuteronomy, the Lord described the role of the Old Testament prophet, "And I will put my words in his mouth, and he shall speak to them all that I command him"(18:18). Because we are now blessed to have the canon of Scripture, the parallel today is knowing the Word of God and speaking it in appropriate circumstances.

*Revisit Deborah's interaction with Barak recorded in Judges 4:6–10.*

What is the essence of what she said to him in verse 6?

_____

_____

_____

_____

_____

Remember, Deborah was a prophetess appointed by God. What does that teach us about the words she spoke to Barak?

_____

_____

_____

_____

_____

Deborah relayed a message that Barak was to recruit an army and lead the Israelites against the Canaanite armies. At first glance, Deborah may not appear soft. These were bold statements she was making! But look again. Deborah simply reminded Barak of the word of the Lord.

> "Has not the LORD, the God of Israel, commanded you, 'Go, gather your men at Mount Tabor, taking 10,000 from the people of Naphtali and the people of Zebulun. And I will draw out Sisera, the general of Jabin's army, to meet you by the river Kishon with his chariots and his troops, and I will give him into your hand'?" (vv. 6–7)

Go back and circle the word "I" in this passage. Is this referring to Deborah? How do you know?

_____

_____

_____

Perhaps Deborah's softness is most evident in what she did *not* do. She didn't command Barak or tell him what to do. She did not berate Barak. She didn't repeat herself over and over. She didn't take command of Barak's army. She wasn't grasping for control. She was fulfilling her role as a prophetess, trusting God's authority and sovereignty over the whole situation. Deborah's responsibility was to deliver the message. Barak was free to take the message or disregard it.

If you listed synonyms for "soft," you might write: not hard, yielding readily to touch, flexible, pliable, delicate, graceful, not loud, quietly pleasant, calm, gentle, kind, tender, compassionate, or sympathetic.

*Read Judges 4:8–9.* Do you see evidence of "softness" from Deborah in this interaction? Explain.

_____

_____

_____

_____

_____

_____

The New Testament uses the word "weaker" to reinforce that women are the softer, more vulnerable ones. That does not imply that women are inferior to men. However, generally speaking, women are physically and emotionally more tender and are thus to be treated with greater care. According to 1 Peter 3:7, God expects men to honor their wives for this beautiful feminine trait. He warns husbands not to treat women like "one of the guys." God expects men to handle women like Swarovski crystal and not like Bridgestone tires!

The world has programmed women to disdain "softness." We are encouraged to be tough and even hard. Though Deborah was faithful to relay God's words, she was not demanding or harsh. She's a reminder that the world's model of womanhood misses out on the beauty of who God created us to be.

What are some ways Deborah could have handled the situation that would have been more tough than tender?

_____

_____

_____

Have there been times when you have tried to exert control over a situation instead of leaving the result up to God? What have been the results?

_____

_____

_____

_____

# Day 5: *Take It Home; Make It Personal*

*Read Proverbs 31:10–31.*

Deborah is just one of many examples Scripture gives us of women of virtue. Proverbs 31 outlines another example. One commentator has called this passage "a looking glass for ladies." [4] It provides a vivid description of a woman of God, a virtuous woman, a woman of influence that we can look into and reflect on our own womanhood.

Consider the definition of valor.

> *Valor: Strength of mind or spirit that enables a person to encounter danger with firmness: personal bravery.* [5]

What evidence of valor do you see in the description of the Proverbs 31 woman?

_____

_____

_____

What evidence of valor do you see in the life of Deborah?

_____

_____

_____

Do you see yourself as a woman of valor? Why or why not?

_____

_____

_____

It is tempting to look at these passages and feel discouraged; sometimes the women in Scripture can feel like an impossible ideal that we can never live up to. *Revisit Proverbs 31:10.* Write it out below.

_____

_____

_____

The Hebrew word used here for "wife", can refer to a wife or a woman. The principle can apply to happily married women, unmarried women, women who may not have a strong marriage or see themselves as an "excellent" wife, and every woman in between.

This kind of womanhood is rare but not impossible. *Any woman who is a child of God can be a woman of conviction and courage.* Any woman who is a child of God can be like these women because Jesus lives in us and He is shaping us into His image. This isn't a formula we are forced to try to live out in our own strength. As we're filled with the Holy Spirit, we can be the kind of woman we see modeled in Scripture.

Some translations use the word "excellent" in verse 10. Others use "virtuous" or "a wife of noble character." The word *virtuous* or *excellent* is a difficult word to translate from the original Hebrew language. It's a word that has to do with strength. It is often translated "army" or "wealth" and is describing a woman of moral fortitude, a woman whose character is strong.

Did you ever get the impression that biblical womanhood meant weak womanhood? What (or who) gave you that idea?

_____

_____

_____

_____

_____

The world would have us think that a godly woman is a woman who gets run over: she never has any opinions, never has any thoughts, never says anything. This caricature doesn't line up with Scripture. A godly woman is a strong woman. She is capable. *She is a woman of influence.*

As you consider the examples of Deborah and the Proverbs 31 woman, what character traits do you see in them that you know God has also developed in you?

_____

_____

_____

_____

_____

What character traits do you see in them that you would like God to develop more in you?

_____

_____

_____

_____

Neither Judges 4–5 nor Proverbs 31 describes a perfect woman. These are not ideals meant to make us feel insecure or discouraged by our own inadequacies. Both are examples of the kind of strength we can have when we allow our identity to be shaped by God's Word.

## AN EVEN BIGGER LOOKING GLASS

*Read James 1:22–25.*

Draw a picture of the metaphor used to describe God's Word in this passage.

If Proverbs 31 is a "looking glass," think of it like the tiny compact mirror that may be tucked away in your purse. To see the bigger picture of who God created us to be, we need all of God's Word. *The whole Bible is a full-length, 360-degree mirror. In it, we can rightly see ourselves and rightly see the character of God so we can reflect Him to the world around us.* To live as women of valor, with strength, courage, and conviction, we need to be women defined by God's Word—not by the cultural messages of womanhood that swirl around us.

Like Deborah, our identities must be shaped by who God has called us to be. To wrap up this week's study, look up the following passages. Next to each one, write a description of the identity assigned to you by God's Word using "I am" statements.

JOHN 1:12       "I AM..."

1 CORINTHIANS 3:16       "I AM..."

2 CORINTHIANS 5:17       "I AM..."

EPHESIANS 2:10       "I AM..."

COLOSSIANS 3:3       "I AM..."

1 THESSALONIANS 1:4       "I AM..."

1 PETER 2:9       "I AM..."

Spend time meditating on and memorizing the following verse this week:

God chose what is low & despised in the world, even things that are not, to bring to nothing things that are, so that no human being might boast in the presence of God.

1 CORINTHIANS 1:28-29

# Week 3

*Big Idea:* GOD OFTEN CHOOSES AND USES UNEXPECTED INSTRUMENTS TO ACCOMPLISH HIS PURPOSES.

No one expected a teenager from Iowa to earn the bronze star.

Roland Baber was just seventeen when he enlisted in the United States Army. He left the small farming community where he grew up in the rearview mirror and shipped off to basic training, then overseas to Europe to fight in the Second World War.

At just five feet four inches tall, Roland didn't look like a warrior. His small stature matched his meek and easygoing nature. No one was more surprised than Roland when a routine scouting mission rustled up twelve Nazi soldiers hiding in the German underbrush. Though he was unarmed and unassuming, Roland single-handedly captured all of the enemy soldiers and marched them back, single file, to his base. Hidden in the sleeve of the coat of one of the Nazi officers were top secret papers with valuable intel, discovered by Roland's commanding officer. Upon his return to the States, Roland was awarded the prestigious bronze star for his bravery. [1]

The Bible is full of stories of unexpected heroes. A stuttering nomad led God's people out of slavery. A young shepherd with a slingshot slew an intimidating giant. Most significantly, *a humble Savior went to war with sin and death so that we could be saved.*

Judges 4–6 reads like a who's who of unexpected warriors. From Deborah to Barak to Jael, none of the players in this story were likely to be given a medal of valor, at least not from a human perspective. May their stories point you to the real hero of this story, of every story, God our Conquering King.

# Day 1: *Our Weakness, His Glory*

*Read Judges 6–7.*

For verse after verse, chapter after chapter, the book of Judges describes unlikely men and women, hand-selected by God to be used in *His story* of delivering His people.

Consider Gideon as an example. God raised Gideon up as a deliverer after Deborah. *Revisit Judges 6:12*. How does the angel of the Lord describe Gideon?

_____

_____

_____

_____

Based on what you've learned about the virtue of valor already in this study, what kind of man do you expect Gideon to be? Circle all words that apply.

heroic
easily intimidated
*brave* wimpy
corageous
*bold*
*nervous* resolute
COMPLIANT
weak *fearful* timid

According to Judges 6:11–18, what was Gideon actually like?

_____

_____

_____

_____

_____

Why do you think the angel described Gideon as a "mighty man of valor"?

_____

_____

_____

_____

_____

_____

_____

Reluctantly, Gideon rose to the assignment and the identity that God gave him. According to Judges 7:2, why did God choose to use such weak vessels for Israel's deliverance?

_____

_____

_____

_____

_____

_____

_____

Let's revisit the twelve judges described throughout the book. Look up the verses listed beneath some of the judges' names, and write down any weaknesses described.

1. OTHNIEL

Judges 3:7


2. EHUD

3. SHAMGAR

4. DEBORAH AND BARAK

Judges 4:8


5. GIDEON

Judges 6:11–18

6. TOLA

7: JAIR

8: JEPHTHAH

Judges 11:1–3; 29–36

**Judges 12:8-9**

**Judges 16:1-6**

Can you think of other examples from Scripture where God used someone weak to accomplish something big? Make a list.

_____

_____

_____

_____

_____

_____

_____

_____

God doesn't usually choose those we consider to be most qualified for the job. He often chooses people like Gideon, those who think they are utterly unqualified for the job—and in many cases they are. As a result, God gets the glory for the outcome.

The apostle Paul wrote about this in 1 Corinthians 1:26–31. Read Paul's words and write his main point in your own words.

_____

_____

_____

Have you seen God use your weakness for His glory? Write about it below.

_____

_____

_____

_____

Though Scripture doesn't list the weaknesses of all of the judges in this era, we know that every judge, including Deborah, was an imperfect instrument. Anything that is human is frail and flawed, fragile and weak. But God, who could just do the job Himself if He wished, often chooses to use human instruments, and they're usually not the people we would expect.

*Circle back to Judges 4:3, 6–7.* Underline the description of Israel's troops. Circle the description of Sisera's troops.

> Then the people of Israel cried out to the LORD for help, for he had 900 chariots of iron and he oppressed the people of Israel cruelly for twenty years. . . .
>
> She sent and summoned Barak the son of Abinoam from Kedesh-naphtali and said to him, "Has not the Lord, the God of Israel, commanded you, 'Go, gather your men at Mount Tabor, taking 10,000 from the people of Naphtali and the people of Zebulun. And I will draw out Sisera, the general of Jabin's army, to meet you by the river Kishon with his chariots and his troops, and I will give him into your hand'?"

Under Barak's leadership, God used an army of men on foot to defeat the Canaanite army. Though they had fought other battles to secure the Promised Land, these were not military men. In contrast, the Canaanites were vicious and were armed with a fleet of 900 iron chariots.

God was saying, in essence, "I don't need chariots to overcome chariots." Instead, He used citizens on foot to accomplish the task. He continues to use those who would be considered unqualified in His battle to win hearts and minds from the enemy so that He gets all of the glory.

To wrap up today's study, meditate on 1 Corinthians 1:26–31. As you consider Paul's words, reflect on how God's glory is revealed through your weakness and what it means to "boast in the Lord" (1 Cor. 1:31).

# Day 2: *Barak: A Reluctant General?*

*Revisit Judges 4:6–10.*

Based on these verses, create a profile of Barak.

FATHER'S NAME:


HOMETOWN:


That's not a lot of information to go on. We don't know anything about Barak's childhood, his marital status, whether or not he had kids, his work history, why God chose him to lead Israel in this battle, or what kind of man he was.

Based on this limited snapshot of Barak, what assumptions do you make about his character?

_____

_____

*Reread Judges 4:6.* What can we assume from Deborah's words, "Has not the LORD, the God of Israel, commanded you?"

_____

_____

_____

Did Barak miss the Lord's message to go to war against Sisera? Did he willfully ignore it? Was he willing to obey, but slow in doing so? Was he a man of faith or fear? Based on the text, we simply don't know.

Go back to the map on page 8:

- Draw a little house near Barak's hometown of Kedesh-naphtali.
- Put a star on the place where God instructed Barak to initiate a battle with Sisera.
- Make a mental note of how far Barak lived from Deborah.

Scripture doesn't reveal the reason that Barak insisted Deborah go with him to the battle. It could have been because he was scared. It could have been an expression of unbelief. Or, because Barak knew Deborah was a woman who walked with God, he may have wanted the presence of God to be with Him in the battle, knowing he could not win this fight in his own strength.

Does Barak asking a woman to join him in the battle seem like a step of strength or weakness to you? Explain.

_____

_____

_____

_____

_____

What does Deborah tell Barak in Judges 4:9? Write down her words.

_____

_____

_____

_____

_____

We could assume that God took the glory for the battle away from Barak as a punishment for wrong motives, but as we've already learned God intentionally uses weak vessels so that *He can get the glory*.

Barak likely assumed that the woman God planned to "sell Sisera into the hand of" was Deborah. As the story unfolds, we'll learn that the hand actually belonged to a different unlikely vessel, but even so, Barak knew that he would not get the glory for the battle. Yet, assured that Deborah would accompany him, Barak obeyed the word of the Lord delivered through Deborah. What does this reveal about his character? Write your thoughts below.

_____

_____

_____

_____

_____

_____

*Judges 4:12–16* fills in some details about the kind of man Barak was. Read these verses and jot down any notes about Barak.

_____

_____

_____

_____

How did Sisera respond when he heard that Barak was on the move (vv. 12–13)?

_____

_____

_____

_____

How many men followed Barak into battle?

_____

Since the general of the Canaanite army responded to Barak's movements, we can assume Barak was a military man, involved with the Israeli military. Because ten thousand foot soldiers followed him into battle, we can assume he was a leader of men. Did he obey the Lord's instructions recorded in verses 6–7?

_____

Barak seems to have been a reluctant leader. Yet ultimately he chose to obey the word of the Lord and to fight against the enemies of Israel, even knowing he would not get the honor for doing so.

Though God wants us to obey right away and all the way, He often uses even our reluctant obedience.

• Consider Moses who expressed his insecurity about his speech (Ex. 4:10), yet God used him to lead the nation of Israel out of slavery in Egypt (Ex. 5:1).
• Remember Gideon who told an angel he was weak and afraid (Judg. 6:15), but God used him to defeat the Midianites.
• Reflect on King David's words, "Who am I, O Lord GOD, and what is my house, that you have brought me thus far?" (2 Sam. 7:18).

To wrap up today's study, reflect on a time when you were fearful or reluctant yet chose to obey the Lord. How did He bless and use you in spite of your hesitancy?

_____

_____

_____

_____

_____

_____

# Day 3: *Jael: Worthy of Praise?*

*Read Judges 4:17–24.*

When God promises the victory, *He delivers.*

*Revisit Judges 4:16.* On the map on page 8, draw a line from the Kishon River, where the battle between Barak and Sisera's armies began, and Harosheth-hagoyim, where the battle ended.

What is the significance of Harosheth-hagoyim? (Hint: Judges 4:2)

_____

_____

_____

Though the enemy had chariots and God's army was on foot, under the leadership of Barak with the encouragement of Deborah, the Israelite army drove the Canaanites back to where they came from and slayed them, down to the last soldier. *Circle back to Judges 1:27–36.* What is the significance of Barak carrying out God's orders so thoroughly?

_____

_____

_____

_____

Who escaped (4:17)?

_____

_____

Here, the plot of the story twists toward another woman of influence. Like Barak and Deborah, there is more we don't know about Jael than what we do know for sure, based on Scripture. But we are given enough details to form a basic profile.

HUSBAND'S NAME: _____ FROM _____

The Kenites were not a part of God's chosen people. The most famous Kenite was Jethro, Moses' father-in-law (Judg. 1:16) and a Midanite (Ex. 2:11–22).

According to Judges 4:11, where did Jael and her family live?

_____

_____

_____

Draw her tent on the map on page 8.

What does verse 17 reveal about the relationship between Jael's family and the enemies of Israel?

_____

_____

_____

Jael's household had apparently declared neutrality, adopting the position, "We're not on either side." Because the Canaanites were such a formidable force, this may have seemed like a matter of survival. Jael was not involved in the battle. Her family members were not involved in the battle. She was in her tent on the day Sisera's army was destroyed, likely tending to her routine daily tasks. (Keep in mind, this was long before the age of modern technology when news of the battle and its outcome could have reached her quickly.)

According to verse 18, how did Jael initially respond to Sisera?

_____

_____

_____

Jael's hospitality soon took a violent turn. When she welcomed Sisera into her tent, did Jael have a plot in her mind to kill him? Was she luring him into a trap? Or did she genuinely welcome him one moment and respond to a prompting from the Lord in the next? We don't know. There are parts about this passage that leave us with unanswered questions.

When you are struggling to understand a passage of Scripture, what is your typical response?

_____

_____

_____

_____

_____

Pause now and ask the Holy Spirit to help you rightly see God's character in the next part of this story. Write out your prayer below.

_____

_____

_____

_____

_____

Underline what Jael did next according to the verses below.

> And Jael came out to meet Sisera and said to him, "Turn aside, my lord; turn aside to me; do not be afraid." So he turned aside to her into the tent, and she covered him with a rug. And he said to her, "Please give me a little water to drink, for I am thirsty." So she opened a skin of milk and gave him a drink and covered him. And he said to her, "Stand at the opening of the tent, and if any man comes and asks you, 'Is anyone here?' say, 'No.'"
>
> But Jael the wife of Heber took a tent peg, and took a hammer in her hand. Then she went softly to him and drove the peg into his temple until it went down into the ground while he was lying fast asleep from weariness. So he died.
>
> And behold, as Barak was pursuing Sisera, Jael went out to meet him and said to him, "Come, and I will show you the man whom you are seeking." So he went in to her tent, and there lay Sisera dead, with the tent peg in his temple. (vv. 18–22)

As gruesome as this part of the story is, as unthinkable as it may be from our perspective, Jael's act became a part of the praise song of God's people. *Read Judges 5:24–27.* How did God's people feel about what Jael did?

_____

_____

_____

_____

_____

Jael's act became a part of the praise hymn the children of Israel sang after the victory was won. **They celebrated the fact that Jael sided with God and against His enemies. That was something God found praiseworthy.**

Jael who was at work in the tent won as rich a blessing as Barak who fought on the battlefield. She was at home, doing what God gave her to do in the moment, and she got as much reward, as much commendation, as much blessing as Barak did for leading ten thousand soldiers into battle.

What "ordinary" things has God placed into your hand to do today? Make a list.

_____

_____

_____

_____

God won't likely bring an enemy general to your doorstep today, but He will bring opportunities for you to make a difference by standing up against the lies and influence of the enemy. He will give you opportunities to stand with the people of God. **As you are doing what God called you to do, wherever it is and whatever it is, you play into God's plan, too. Like Jael and Barak, your reward will be great. All God asks is that you do your part.**

To wrap up today's study, reflect on these thoughts from Charles Spurgeon about the passage we've studied today:

The Lord can still use feeble instrumentalities. Why not me? He may use persons who are not commonly called to great public engagements. Why not you? The woman who slew the enemy of Israel was no Amazon but a wife who tarried in her tent. She was no orator but a woman who milked the cows and made butter. **May not the Lord use any one of us to accomplish His purpose?**

Somebody may come to the house today, even as Sisera came to Jael's tent. Be it ours not to slay him, but to save him. Let us receive him with great kindness and then bring forth the blessed truth of salvation by the Lord Jesus, our great Substitute, and press home the command "Believe and live." Who knoweth but some stout-hearted sinner may be slain by the gospel today! [2]

# Day 4: *Jesus: Unlikely Deliverer?*

*Read Matthew 1:18–25.*

The nation of Israel didn't stop praying for deliverance after the account of Deborah and Barak. God's children cried out to the Lord for help over and over during the period of judges and over and over in the centuries that followed. Through the prophets, God promised a Messiah, but when He came, wrapped in swaddling clothes and lying in a manger, many missed the unlikely Savior.

*The Bible is a book about God.* As we study Scripture, it is helpful to train ourselves to ask two fundamental questions about each passage:

- What does this tell me about God's character?
- How does this point me to the gospel?

Let's reflect on what we've learned so far. What does Deborah's story reveal about the character of God?

_____

_____

_____

_____

What about the gospel? To consider how Israel's deliverance from the Canaanites in Judges 4–5 connects to Christ's death, burial, and resurrection recorded in the Gospels, let's consider the judges again. What made them unlikely deliverers?

_____

_____

Revisit the cycle of the Four Ds we outlined in week 1 below.

• D_____
• D_____
• D_____
• D_____

What does all of humanity need to be delivered from?

_____

Use the passages below to consider Jesus. Next to each one, write what made Him an unlikely deliverer.

ISAIAH 53:2

MATTHEW 1:18-23

MARK 6:3

PHILIPPIANS 2:6-8

*Skim the list of Jesus' genealogy recorded in Matthew 1:1–17.* This list of names represents the family tree of Jesus, humanly speaking, but it is also a who's who of unlikely heroes. Abraham was prone to faithlessness and known to lie (Gen. 20:1–18). Rahab was a prostitute (Josh. 2:1). David was a shepherd boy (1 Sam. 17:34) turned adulterer (2 Sam. 11). Zerubbabel was a political refugee (Ezra 2:1–2).

These were not necessarily people who possessed unusual natural gifts. *God rarely uses human qualifications or strength to achieve divine intervention.* Yet Jesus and Deborah's similar humble position is not the only connection between her story and the gospel.

Use the chart below to compare and contrast Deborah's story and the gospel story.

| ISRAEL'S ENEMY<br>JUDGES 4:2 | OUR ENEMY<br>EPHESIANS 6:12 |
| --- | --- |
| | |

| ISRAEL'S HEART CRY<br>JUDGES 4:3 | OUR HEART CRY<br>PSALM 51:2 |
| --- | --- |
| | |

| WEAPON USED TO<br>DEFEAT SISERA<br>JUDGES 4:21 | WEAPON USED TO<br>DEFEAT SATAN<br>HEBREWS 2:14 |
| --- | --- |
| | |

| RESULT OF ISRAEL'S DELIVERANCE JUDGES 5:31 | RESULT OF OUR DELIVERANCE COLOSSIANS 1:19-20 |
| --- | --- |
| | |

Are there gospel connections in Judges 4–5 you've not noticed before? Write about them below.

_____

_____

_____

Jesus, our unlikely Redeemer, came to deliver us from our ongoing pattern of disobedience, which required divine discipline and resulted in our desperation. While God's appointed judges led God's people to a temporary deliverance, their mark on human history is like an ellipsis … simply an interlude before the next Four D cycle began. *But through His death on the cross, Jesus is the exclamation point.* Because of the gospel, we are delivered once and for all from the eternal consequences of our sin by His blood. Jael dealt a gruesome death blow to Sisera's temple with her tent peg. Jesus, our Savior, with nail-pierced hands and feet, dealt a gory death blow to sin with His sacrifice.

To wrap up today's study, ask the Lord to help you see the gospel more clearly throughout all of Scripture.

## Day 5: *Take It Home; Make It Personal*

*Read 1 Corinthians 15:9–11.*

The kingdom of God is not an episode of *American Idol.* Disciples are not chosen based on talent or beauty. Leaders are not chosen based on strength or charisma. World changers are not elected by popular vote. We operate differently than the world.

Draw a picture of how Jesus described this principle in Matthew 20:16.

The apostle Paul epitomized this truth and he knew it. Before his dramatic conversion, Paul terrorized Christians in the name of religious zeal. He approved of the execution of saints (Acts 8:1). He personally entered the homes of Christians and dragged men and women to prison for following Jesus (v. 3). But after a dramatic encounter with Christ, Paul moved from persecutor to proclaimer, declaring the gospel with unmatched boldness until he was martyred for his faith.

Like Deborah, Barak, and Jael, Paul was an unlikely instrument of God's grace. Keep his story in mind as you consider the words he wrote in 2 Corinthians 5:11–21 below. As you read:

• Underline words or phrases that describe our calling as Christians.
• Circle words or phrases that indicate what qualifies us to carry out our calling.

> Therefore, knowing the fear of the Lord, we persuade others. But what we are is known to God, and I hope it is known also to your conscience. We are not commending ourselves to you again but giving you cause to boast about us, so that you may be able to answer those who boast about outward appearance and not about what is in the heart. For if we are beside ourselves, it is for God; if we

are in our right mind, it is for you. For the love of Christ controls us, because we have concluded this: that one has died for all, therefore all have died; and he died for all, that those who live might no longer live for themselves but for him who for their sake died and was raised.

From now on, therefore, we regard no one according to the flesh. Even though we once regarded Christ according to the flesh, we regard him thus no longer. Therefore, if anyone is in Christ, he is a new creation. The old has passed away; behold, the new has come. All this is from God, who through Christ reconciled us to himself and gave us the ministry of reconciliation; that is, in Christ God was reconciling the world to himself, not counting their trespasses against them, and entrusting to us the message of reconciliation. Therefore, we are ambassadors for Christ, God making his appeal through us. We implore you on behalf of Christ, be reconciled to God. For our sake he made him to be sin who knew no sin, so that in him we might become the righteousness of God.

What is the "ministry of reconciliation" that Paul referred to?

_____

_____

_____

This calling goes beyond healing human relationships. We are to be ambassadors of the gospel, witnesses that because of Jesus, it is possible for sinners to be reconciled to God. Those who don't know Christ are still locked in the cycle of the Four Ds: disobedience still leads to divine discipline, resulting in human desperation. *There are so many people who need to know that Christ offers deliverance from this painful cycle.*

Why do you think Deborah shared God's message so boldly with Barak?

_____

_____

_____

What was at stake if she refused?

_____

_____

_____

What prevents you from sharing the truth of the gospel boldly with others?

_____

_____

_____

What is at stake if you refuse?

_____

_____

_____

Do you feel like an unlikely gospel ambassador? Perhaps your story is messy or you have a timid personality. Maybe you doubt your knowledge of Scripture or worry you won't be able to answer questions others may raise.

One way Deborah's story can inspire us is as an example of a woman who humbly embraced God's call on her life. Though she saw herself as a mother, she was willing to say "Yes, Lord" and she became a mouthpiece for God's truth.

We can be like Deborah by having a heart attitude that declares, "Lord, if my life leads to the deliverance of others and plays a part in their reconciliation to You, it's not because I am more spiritual or more gifted than someone else. It is because you chose to use someone who is weak and needy."

When God uses you—as a wife, as a mom, a friend, a neighbor, in your workplace, your church, your family—**as an instrument of touching and changing lives, and when spiritual battles are fought and won—you can't take the credit. God is the One who changes hearts. God gets the glory.**

To wrap up this week's study, rewrite 2 Corinthians 5:11–21 in your own words, focusing on God's calling on your life and what qualifies you to fulfill that calling.

_____

_____

_____

_____

_____

_____

_____

_____

_____

_____

_____

_____

_____

_____

_____

_____

_____

_____

_____

_____

_____

Spend time meditating on and memorizing the following verse this week:

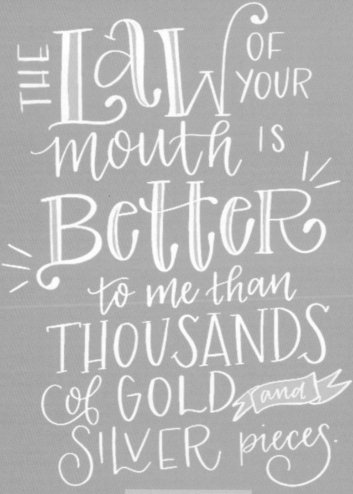

THE LAW OF YOUR mouth IS BETTER to me than THOUSANDS of GOLD and SILVER pieces.

PSALM 119:72

# Week 4

*Big Idea:* A WOMAN WHO EMBRACES GOD'S
WORD IS A WOMAN OF INFLUENCE.

The Bible was written before bulldozers. Consider how that fact deepens the meaning of these verses:

> The LORD is my rock and my fortress and my deliverer,
>     my God, my rock, in whom I take refuge. ( PSALM  18:2)
>
> For who is God, but the LORD?
>     And who is a rock, except our God? ( PSALM  18:31)
>
> Be to me a rock of refuge,
>     to which I may continually come;
>     you have given the command to save me
>     for you are my rock and my fortress. ( PSALM  71:3)

For the psalmist, a rock was permanent and unmovable—unable to be shaken by people or circumstances.

Deborah showed remarkable confidence in the Word of God. She knew that even as the winds of war swirled through the nation of Israel, her footing was secure. She could stand on the Rock of God's truth and character. Deborah's confidence inspired others to turn to her for wise, righteous guidance, and it emboldened her to accompany Barak as he charged into battle against a wicked king.

As you continue exploring Deborah's story this week, may your heart find steady footing on the Rock of God's Word.

# Day 1: *God Speaks through His Word*

*Read Psalm 119.*

Psalm 119 is the longest psalm in the Bible. With 176 verses, it is longer than some entire books of the Bible. This psalm is an acrostic poem of twenty-two stanzas, following the letters of the Hebrew alphabet. Within each stanza, each verse begins with the same Hebrew letter.

Consider the early verses of this psalm. Is it clear who wrote it?

_____

_____

Unlike many psalms, the author of Psalm 119 is unnamed. Most scholars believe that David penned these words as an opus he worked on for his entire life. Others believe it was written later in the history of Israel. [1] The name of the writer is inconsequential; it is the heart of this psalm that matters most.

Summarize the theme of Psalm 119 in a single sentence below.

_____

_____

_____

_____

How does verse 72 describe God's law?

_____

_____

_____

_____

_____

What are some of the treasures you've discovered as you've studied the Scriptures?

_____

_____

_____

Match the references below with the corresponding benefit of knowing Scripture.

Psalm 119:43                     Strength in times of sorrow


Psalm 119:9                      Hope


Psalm 119:29                     Light and understanding


Psalm 119:130                    False ways are put away


Psalm 119:28                     Songs in times of sojourning


Psalm 119:54                     Keep your way pure

One word the psalmist used repeatedly throughout Psalm 119 is "delight." What does it mean to delight in God's Word? As you search your own heart, does "delight" accurately describe your attitude toward Scripture? Explain.

_____

_____

_____

_____

*Read James 2:22–25.*

James builds on the psalmist's premise by pointing out it's not enough to simply delight in Scripture, like we might delight in a beautiful flower or a picturesque sunset. We must move from delighting to *doing*.

What does it mean to be a doer of God's Word?

_____

_____

_____

*Go back to Judges 4:4.* Do you see evidence that Deborah delighted in and acted upon God's Word? Explain.

_____

_____

_____

_____

_____

Remember, what was the God-given job description of a prophet? (See Deuteronomy 18:18–19 for review.)

Deborah's role in the nation of Israel was to teach, warn, and encourage *according to God's words, not her words*. In order to speak God's words, Deborah had to know God's words.

*Look closely at Judges 4:7.* Do you see more evidence that Deborah knew and responded to God's Word? Explain.

_____

_____

_____

_____

Deborah lived in a different part of God's redemptive timeline, before Pentecost, when the Holy Spirit came to live in the hearts of Christ's followers (1 Cor. 6:19) and before God's Word was available to His children in the written, canonized book we have now. Yet Deborah still heard and responded to the Word of the Lord.

Look up the following passages and record how God speaks to us through His Word.

PSALM 119:105

2 TIMOTHY 3:16-17

HEBREWS 1:1-2

HEBREWS 4:12

2 PETER 1:19-21

You may read Deborah's story and wonder how you can emulate her. While God may not have gifted you in the same way He gifted Deborah, you can be a woman of influence who hears God through His Word and responds, calling others to do the same.

To wrap up today's study, choose one stanza of Psalm 119 and rewrite it in your own words as a way to affirm your desire to delight in and be a doer of God's Word.

_____

_____

_____

_____

_____

_____

_____

_____

_____

_____

## Day 2: *Fully Convinced of God's Promises*

*Read Numbers 13.*

Before Israel dwelled in the land of Cannan in the days of Deborah, they came to its borders and struggled to take God at His Word.

Try to put yourself in the spies' shoes. Your people had been moving toward this moment with great expectation. Now, at the very cusp of the land God had promised to your people, you were the first to set foot on the soil so many had been pining for.

Everything seemed new and strange. Your eyes saw grapes the size of boulders and enemies just as impressive.

After forty days of exploring, your job was to report back to your friends and family. They hung on your every word, desperate for a sign that their wait was finally over. You had one choice: trust God's promises or succumb to the fear of the unknown.

*Read Genesis 12:1–7.* Write down the specific promises God made to Abraham.

_____

_____

_____

_____

_____

_____

_____

God confirmed the promise He had made to Abraham's son Isaac and to Isaac's son Jacob. Write down God's promises found in the verses below.

GENESIS 26:3

GENESIS 28:13

Abraham's descendants became the nation of Israel. Their temporary enslavement in Egypt did not stop God's promise. When He delivered them *from* slavery, He also delivered them to Abraham's promised territory.

When the twelve spies returned to the assembly to report back from their scouting mission, they brought good news and bad news. What did they report?

| GOOD NEWS | BAD NEWS |
| --- | --- |
| | |

One spy spoke up and encouraged God's people to rush in and take the land. Why do you think Caleb was so confident?

_____

_____

_____

*Read Numbers 14:1–4.* Did the people share Caleb's confidence? Explain.

_____

_____

_____

_____

_____

Ultimately, this is not a passage about whether or not God's people agreed with one spy. This is about whether or not they trusted God's promises. God promised that He would give them the land. He confirmed that promise across many generations and hardships. Still, they trusted their fear instead. It's a pattern that continued into the days of Deborah.

*Go back to Judges 4:7.* What promise did Deborah declare?

_____

_____

_____

*Revisit Judges 4:3.* Humanly speaking, did Deborah have reasons to doubt God's promise? Explain.

_____

_____

_____

_____

Do you see evidence that Deborah doubted or trusted God's promises? Explain.

_____

_____

_____

_____

*Read 2 Peter 1:3–4.* What words are used to describe God's promises?

_____

God's promises are not precious simply because they make us feel good. *They are precious because they are true.*

*Read Romans 4:13–25.* This passage describes Abraham, to whom God promised that He would set aside a nation of people and give them a fruitful land. Abraham's faith was demonstrated in his trust that God would follow through. He was ***fully convinced*** that God would do what He promised (v. 21). Because Caleb was fully convinced of the same, he was willing to charge into a land filled with intimidating enemies.

Because Deborah was fully convinced, she encouraged Barak to go after Sisera. When we are fully convinced, we are able to live as women of influence who obey God's Word boldly and without fear.

To wrap up today's study, meditate on the precious and very great promises of God. Choose a few from the list below or review some of your favorite promises found in Scripture.

2 CHRONICLES 30:9

PSALM 37:4

ISAIAH 54:10

ROMANS 8:38-39

2 TIMOTHY 2:13

HEBREWS 9:13-14

JAMES 1:5

# Day 3: *The Word in Us*

*Read James 1:19–21.*

Implant.

What images does that word stir within you? Maybe it sounds bionic, like a tracking chip inserted into your beloved pet. Perhaps it sounds permanent, like a dental device embedded into your mouth. Those images help us consider what James meant when he wrote that God's Word should be implanted into our hearts, minds, and lives.

Using an online Bible dictionary, look up the word "implant." Write down what you find.

_____

_____

_____

How is James encouraging us to interact with our Bibles?

_____

_____

_____

James described the "implanted word" right before he encouraged Christ's followers to be doers of the Word. The big idea is that our obedience to Scripture is not simply strict adherence to a to-do list but rather an outflow of the fact that the truth of Scripture is embedded deep within us.

Do you know a Word-filled woman? Briefly describe her below.

_____

_____

_____

_____

Jump back into Deborah's story, revisiting Judges 4:6. How did Deborah know what to say to Barak?

_____

_____

_____

_____

This was a big assignment! Deborah needed to call for the leader of her nation's army and tell him to take on a massive and battle-ready enemy.

Does it seem like this was the first time Deborah heard from the Lord? Explain.

_____

_____

_____

*Read Colossians 3:16.* Write the command given in this verse above the horizontal line. Write the calls to action above the diagonal lines. (Hint: they are all ing words.)

TEACHING

COMMAND

_____

THANKFULNESS

Deborah's day in, day out likely felt unremarkable. She practiced listening to and obeying the Lord as she sat under a palm tree, administering righteous judgment according to God's law. As she listened to the Lord and responded, His Word was implanted deeper and deeper into her heart and life. As a result, she did just what the author of Colossians encouraged us to do: she taught and admonished others in wisdom, and (as we will see in Judges 5) she sang songs of thankful praise.

Think about the Word-filled woman you described above. How does her love for and commitment to God's Word flow out of her life?

_____

_____

_____

_____

God's Word may not become implanted deeply into your heart as you judge from the base of a palm tree. Instead it will grow amidst the routines of your everyday life as you open your Bible, believe, and respond.

Consider your daily routines. Is God's Word being implanted in your heart each day? Use the sliding scales below for reflection.

I read God's Word daily.

*Never*          *Sometimes*          *Always*

1     2     3     4     5     6     7     8     9     10

I meditate on God's Word often.

*Never*          *Sometimes*          *Always*

1     2     3     4     5     6     7     8     9     10

I listen and respond to biblical teaching.

*Never*          *Sometimes*          *Always*

1     2     3     4     5     6     7     8     9     10

I listen to music based on Scripture.

*Never*                   *Sometimes*                  *Always*

1      2      3      4      5      6      7      8      9      10

I memorize Scripture.

*Never*                   *Sometimes*                  *Always*

1      2      3      4      5      6      7      8      9      10

I strive to know God's Word so I can be a doer of it.

*Never*                   *Sometimes*                  *Always*

1      2      3      4      5      6      7      8      9      10

Just as soldiers train for battle through tasks and drills that may seem mundane, Deborah prepared to encourage God's chosen leader and accompany him and God's people into battle with the basic training of letting God's Word embed itself deeply into her heart.

To wrap up today's study, write out a prayer asking God to show you how to become like Deborah in this way. Ask Him to help you develop habits that will embed His Word more deeply into your life.

_____

_____

_____

_____

_____

_____

_____

_____

# Day 4: *A Woman of Influence*

*Read Judges 4:12–16.*

The day of the battle had arrived. Sisera brought the full force of his army up against the Israelites. They gathered like a dark horde on the bank of the Kishon River.

Picture yourself as Deborah for a moment. Imagine yourself standing side by side with Barak, away from the comforts of home and moments away from the battle. Ten thousand of your countrymen have assembled waiting for the signal that the battle has begun. The energy of the moment is palpable. What do you think you'd be feeling? Write about it below.

_____

_____

_____

_____

Record Deborah's exact words from Judges 4:14 below.

_____

_____

_____

_____

Rewrite Deborah's words in modern language.

_____

_____

_____

_____

As the commander of the Israelite army heading into battle, Barak was strengthened by Deborah's reminder of the promises of God and the assurance that His promises can be trusted.

Deborah believed God. She believed that He was sovereign, that He was powerful, and that God would win the battle. And God used her to infuse faith in the heart of Barak who knew what a huge battle he was facing.

Deborah was a wise woman. Her wisdom flowed out of her delight to hear God's Word and her obedience to do what she heard. She knew God and listened to Him. When she spoke, it was not her own wisdom and ideas that came out but words she had heard and received from the Lord. Because she had confidence in God's Word, people looked to her for answers.

Consider the conversations you've had in the past twenty-four hours. Did your input mostly focus on your ideas and opinions or on God's Word? Reflect below.

_____

_____

_____

_____

_____

Deborah likely had opinions about what Barak should do, but she chose to focus her words on what matters most, God's commands and promises. Our opinions don't matter any more than anyone else's, but when we become women of influence who know God's words and internalize them, live them, and share them with others, people will stop and be influenced to obey His Word.

To whom do you go for wise guidance? Does that person primarily offer you their thoughts and opinions or God's? Explain.

_____

_____

_____

_____

Do people come to you for wise guidance? Explain.

_____

_____

_____

You may think, *I'm not a counselor.* You don't need to be a counselor. You just need to know the Wonderful Counselor, and people need to know that you listen to Him, know His Word, and desire to point them to it. Anyone can go to *The View* to get the world's way of thinking, but do they know to come to you to get the true view—God's way of thinking?

*Review Judges 4:6–10,14.* How did Barak respond to Deborah?

_____

_____

_____

_____

_____

In the big picture, how did Deborah's wise instruction and Barak's response impact the nation of Israel?

_____

_____

_____

_____

_____

*Read Judges 4:15–16.* Compare it with Judges 4:6. Do you see a change in Barak?

_____

_____

_____

What role do you think Deborah played in these changes?

_____

_____

_____

_____

_____

A Word-filled woman is not just a woman of temporary influence; she is a woman of *lasting influence*. Deborah's obedience to God's Word impacted Barak, who impacted the army of Israel, who impacted the entire nation. We're still talking about Deborah's influence today.

To wrap up today's study, fill in the circles below. Write the names or descriptions of the people or groups that you want to influence with godly, Word-filled wisdom. Start with your inner circle, family and friends, and then expand, considering how you hope your life impacts the people around you and even future generations.

# Day 5: *Take It Home; Make It Personal*

*Reread Psalm 119:1–16, 41–48, 97–104, 137–144, and 161–176.*

In his devotional book on the Psalms, Sam Storms says that Psalm 119 shows to us the "mind-blowing beauty, the sin-killing power, and the breathtaking expanse of God's Word."[2] In just this selection of verses, we find at least eight synonyms for God's Word. List them below.

- _____
- _____
- _____
- _____
- _____
- _____
- _____
- _____

These verses also list several adjectives, or descriptors of God's Word. Add what you find to the list started below.

- *Righteous (v. 7)*
- *Sweet (v. 103)*
- 
- 
- 
- 
- 

Throughout the psalm, the writer makes affirmations, resolutions, and petitions, but pulsing through every stanza are statements of adoration and celebration. The words "delight" and "love" are woven throughout. The psalmist loved God's Word. He praised God for its wonder and beauty and sweetness.

Write out the passages below.

PSALM 119:24

PSALM 119:97

PSALM 119:103

Consider Margaret's story. Margaret was a concert violinist who grew up in Bulgaria under a repressive Communist regime. When she was a little girl, the Communists confiscated virtually all the Bibles in the country, but there was an elderly woman in Margaret's town who managed to hide one Bible. It became a treasure shared by all of the believers in that town. Each page, one at a time, was carefully torn out of that Bible and distributed, one by one, to the Christians where Margaret lived. She received one page that included Genesis 16 and 17. Margaret cherished that page and studied it diligently.

In her mid-thirties, Margaret moved to the United States. Shortly after her arrival, Margaret's new friends asked her what she'd like for Christmas. Margaret didn't hesitate. She wanted a Bible! Her friends took her to a Christian bookstore to buy one. It was the first time she had ever seen a complete Bible. She wept for joy. [3]

Why do you think Margaret was so moved by the sight of God's Word?

_____

_____

_____

God's Word is a delight. It truly is a treasure trove. But familiarity can make even the richest, sweetest treasures seem commonplace. Consider, is God's Word your delight? Do you long for it? Or have your affections for God's Word dulled? Write about that below.

_____

_____

_____

_____

_____

We all fight a tendency to turn to things other than God's Word in search of pleasure and joy. In that process, we lose our appetite for the food that truly satisfies. In the list below, circle the three things that tug most strongly at your affections.

• *Technology*
• *Work*
• *Family*
• *Relaxation*
• *Comfort*
• *Social Media*
• *Food*
• *Relationships*
• *Fitness*

How do we find delight in God's Word when our affections are askew? *We read it.* We read the Bible when we feel like reading it; we read it when we don't feel like reading it; we read it until we do feel like reading it.

Soak in it. Marinate in it. Meditate on it.

When you do, your delight for God's Word will return, and you will be battle ready—ready to respond to God's Word when the moment calls for it.

To wrap up this week of study, personalize Jeremiah 15:16 as a prayer.

_____

_____

_____

_____

_____

_____

_____

_____

_____

_____

Spend time meditating on and memorizing the following verse this week:

So GOD created MAN in HIS own image, in the IMAGE of GOD he CREATED him; male and female he CREATED them.

GENESIS 1:27

# Week 5

*Big Idea:* SCRIPTURE CALLS US
TO EMBRACE GOD'S DESIGN.

What would it be like if God were to start a movement among Christian women in our generation? A movement of women who . . .

* love and respond obediently to His Word.
* live out the gospel and proclaim it to others.
* live out their God-given design and calling.

Since the Garden of Eden, women have faced the temptation to abandon God's authority in favor of "personal truth." Ever since Eve disobeyed God's command and reached for the fruit He forbade, a battle has raged in every woman's heart:

* A battle for authority
* A battle for truth
* A battle for trust

Deborah did not reject her God-given design as a woman but instead fought *for* her unique role as an affirmer, receiver, and life-giver. Even as she accompanied Barak and the troops of Israel as they charged into battle against Sisera's army, she waved the white flag of surrender to God, forsaking her own plans for His.

Through her surrender to God, Deborah left a legacy that still inspires us to embrace God's plan for our lives. As you open your Bible this week, may you consider what mark you will leave on the next generation and wave the white flag of surrender to God's good plan.

# Day 1: *Honoring Those Who Lead*

*Read Judges 17:6 and Judges 21:25.*

The book of Judges has a tragic ending. After 300 years and twelve God-appointed judges, Israel's moral fabric was torn, and "everyone did what was right in his own eyes" (21:25).

Describe what it might look like for everyone in a society to do what is "right in his own eyes."

_____

_____

_____

_____

List a few specific examples of this mindset that you see in our world today.

_____

_____

_____

_____

Think back to the cycle of the Four Ds from week 1. What pattern did God's people repeat over and over?

_____

_____

_____

_____

Think about the times in which Deborah lived. Israel was:

• Given over to idolatry.
• Under the thumb of the Canaanites, the ones they were supposed to have conquered.
• Under the disciplining and chastening hand of God.

- Outnumbered and overwhelmed by the enemy.
- Fearful.
- Experiencing low morale.

And, as is often the case when people come under the chastening and disciplining of God, there was a noticeable lack of strong, godly male leadership.

Revist that list. Circle any words or phrases that accurately describe the times in which we live.

The Israelites wanted to be like the godless people and nations around them. They imitated their ways and ended up being slaves to the ones they were imitating. What evidence do you see that the world has enslaved the people of God today?

_____

_____

_____

*Revisit Judges 4:1 and Judges 17:6.* What connections can you make between Israel's rebellion against God's authority and their response to human authority?

Submission to human leadership is meant to be a picture of how we submit to God's authority in our lives (Rom. 13:1–3). God has appointed specific authorities to which we are to yield, and by doing so, we submit to God. Yet because we are sinners, submission is not easy—for any of us.

Consider the following passages. What do we learn in these passages about God-appointed authority in various spheres in our lives and relationships? Write your answers in the space below.

EPHESIANS 5:22-24

EPHESIANS 6:1-4

Barak's initial failure to obey the Lord's command to attack Sisera (Judg. 4:6) seems to indicate that he was hesitant, perhaps even fearful, to take on leadership when it was sorely needed.

*Look up Judges 4:8.* What do you think this verse reveals about Barak's hesitancy to obey God's call to lead?

_____

_____

_____

_____

_____

How did Deborah respond to Barak as the man God raised up to lead Israel into battle?

_____

_____

_____

_____

Deborah did not seek to commandeer Barak's role. She did not belittle him or publicly shame him for his weakness. She approached him with respect and a clear willingness to let him lead. She proactively inspired him to fulfill his *God-given mission.* These responses revealed that Deborah's trust was ultimately in God, not in a person.

Many women today struggle with the reluctance of men to step up and take initiative to lead in difficult situations. How can faith-filled women make a difference in those men?

_____

_____

_____

_____

_____

_____

_____

_____

*Circle back to Judges 1:1.* What big event kicked off the period of the judges?

_____

_____

_____

_____

In Deborah's day, the Israelites were operating without spiritual leadership. By Judges 4, that leadership vacuum led God's people into deep bondage. When they cried out to God for help, He sent a deliverer—Deborah. God put His word in her heart and gave her the responsibility to speak truth.

At this moment in Israel's history, Deborah held a position of influence. God chose Deborah at this specific time to judge and speak His word to His people. The nation of Israel was in spiritual decline. Deborah modeled wise, effective influence by listening and responding to the Lord. As a result, she was respected and honored as God's chosen instrument. God used Deborah's faith and courage—*rooted in both His promises and direction*—to inspire Barak to believe God and to lead an army to overthrow their oppressors.

Consider our culture: do our general attitudes and conversations about leadership reveal anything about the spiritual condition of our nation?

_____

_____

_____

Make it personal: do your own responses and reactions to those God has placed in leadership positions reveal your trust in Him? Why or why not?

_____

_____

_____

_____

_____

_____

_____

To wrap up today's study, make a list of honorable, godly leaders in your world. Start in your home if possible; then consider your workplace, community, church, and nation. Pray for these people to be godly leaders who serve with integrity and lead in accordance with Scripture.

_____

_____

_____

_____

_____

_____

# Day 2: *Submitting to God's Call*

*Read Genesis 1:27–31.*

The first chapter of the Bible outlines truths that are foundational to our understanding of our design.

Write out the verses that correspond with each essential truth.

GENESIS 1:1

**Truth: God created everything.**

GENESIS 1:31

**Truth: God's creation is good.**

GENESIS 1:27

**Truth: God created men and women.**

**Truth: God created men and women in His image.**

The tandem truths that God created everything and that He created man and woman to bear His image are key to understanding His design for manhood and womanhood. Since **God is our Creator, He gets to decide what it means to honor Him.**

Deborah is an example of a woman who honored her Creator. She lived in difficult, desperate times and carried a burden for the condition of God's people. She was blessed with unique gifts and seems to have known more of the Word and ways of God than others around her. She possessed courage grounded in the promises of God. Yet she did not set out to lead the troops into battle for herself. She came alongside the man God had appointed for that task and infused him with courage by her supportive role. We can follow her example by recognizing that as our Designer, God determines when and how He uses us for His purposes.

Remember: who appointed Deborah to be a prophetess?

_____

Whose words did she speak?

_____

The Bible gives us many examples of individuals whom God called for a specific purpose. Match the individuals with the verses that describe their calling from the lists below.

ABRAHAM                          Genesis 12:1-3


MOSES                            Luke 1:8-16


MARY                             Luke 1:26-38


PAUL                             Exodus 3:1-10


SIMON AND ANDREW                 Acts 9:1-9


ZECHARIAH                        Mark 1:16-20


God's Word provides wisdom and direction for serving Him. We may sometimes be tempted to wish we had a different calling or to covet the calling God has given to others. We need to remember that ministry is not a right. Ministry is a calling. God determines who He calls, what responsibilities they are given, and what qualifications are required for specific roles in ministry.

The priesthood in the Old Testament was not a right. God called priests from a specific family line in a particular tribe to serve in this role. The disciples in the New Testament did not run for office or elect themselves. They were ordained by Jesus to join Him in ministry and establish His Church. Can you think of other examples from Scripture where God called individuals or groups for His purposes? List them below.

_____

_____

_____

_____

_____

God has the right to say who does what in His kingdom. We need to study His Word to learn His ways and then accept His plan with meekness, humility, and a submissive heart. No one has the "right" to lead. Our only right is to obey God.

Do you ever chafe at God's plan, wishing for certain ministry opportunities He has not given you? Explain.

_____

_____

_____

Look up the following passages. Next to each one, jot some notes about what God's Word teaches about submitting to His plan.

PROVERBS 3:5-6

ROMANS 8:5-8

Do you see evidence of Deborah being submissive to God's call on her life? Explain.

_____

_____

_____

Is there anything you specifically want to avoid or emulate from her example?

_____

_____

Do you see evidence of Barak being resistant to God's call on his life? Explain.

_____

_____

_____

_____

Is there anything you specifically want to avoid or emulate from his example? Explain.

_____

_____

_____

_____

*Revisit Judges 5:6–7.* How did Deborah describe God's call on her life? What do her words reveal about her perspective on herself and her calling as a woman?

_____

_____

_____

In describing herself as a "mother in Israel," Deborah expressed a heart to embrace her God-created design and to serve Him and others in distinctly feminine ways. Her story illustrates the difference between influence and control. She exerted enormous influence without having to be in control.

Like Deborah, when we serve as female image-bearers of God, we can wield greater influence than if we tried to assume positions God has assigned to men. Deborah was a woman of great courage and faith. But her goal was not to make a name for herself or to lead the charge against the enemies of God. In an era when men and women alike were fearful to act, she affirmed and encouraged the men around her to take the "lead in Israel" (5:2).

To wrap up today's study, imagine you have a female friend who is grappling with the concept of God calling men to lead in their homes and in the church. She says to you, "I just don't get it. Women are no less spiritual, gifted, or capable than men. Why should the husband be the head of the wife and why shouldn't women be able to be pastors and elders and teach men and women in the church, if they have those kinds of gifts?" What advice would you give her based on God's Word? Write out your response in a letter below.

_____

_____

_____

_____

_____

_____

_____

_____

# Day 3: *Arise!*

*Read Judges 4:12–5:12.*

Embracing God's design for womanhood also means celebrating His design for manhood. Trusting and embracing God's design for our identity equips us to lift up and affirm male leadership.

For each of the passages listed below, make observations about Barak's behaviors and attitudes throughout Judges 4–5.

| JUDGES 4:6 | JUDGES 4:8 | JUDGES 4:14 | JUDGES 4:16 |
|---|---|---|---|
| | | | |

What changes do you see in Barak over the course of this story?

_____

_____

_____

*Turn to Hebrews 11.* This chapter of the Bible is often called the "Hall of Faith" as it lists people from the Old Testament who trusted the Lord by faith. List the names recorded in verse 32. Circle the name listed that comes from Judges 4–5.

_____

_____

_____

_____

_____

Why do you think Barak is listed in the "Hall of Faith"?

_____

_____

_____

_____

_____

What role, if any, do you think Deborah played in Barak's faith?

_____

_____

_____

_____

_____

Judges 5 records a victory song Deborah and Barak sang after they defeated Sisera and his army. The lyrics reveal a lot about Deborah's disposition toward Barak.

Write down the words found in verses 2–3 in the space below.

_____

_____

_____

_____

_____

Deborah was faithful in fulfilling her God-given calling. She acted in ways that affirmed and supported God-appointed leadership in others. She communicated a message from the Lord to Barak, encouraging him to step into his God-appointed role as a leader (4:6). She nurtured valor in Barak and created an environment conducive to his fulfilling his God-created calling as a protector and defender of God's people. She was willing to accompany Barak into battle when he insisted he needed her at his side (4:9). When Barak stepped up to lead, Deborah saw it as an occasion to worship the Lord, for Barak was a leader appointed by God (5:9).

Nineteenth Century British pastor John Angell James once said:

> Every woman whether rich or poor, married or single, has a circle of influence within which according to her character, she is exerting a certain amount of power for good or for harm. Every woman, by her virtue or her vice, by her folly or her wisdom, by her levity or her dignity is adding something to our national elevation or degradation. [1]

Every one of us as women is adding something to the condition of our world. We're helping make it a better place, or we are pulling it down. There's no neutral.

Pastor James went on to say,

> A community is not likely to be overthrown where a woman fulfilled her mission, for by the power of her noble heart over the hearts of others, she will raise it from its ruins and restore it again to prosperity and joy. [2]

We see this reality lived out in Deborah. She is an illustration of a true woman, a woman who exerted strong, godly influence in a way that encouraged the men around her to be more godly and to take greater leadership.

*Read 1 Peter 3:1–6.* Summarize these verses in your own words below.

_____

_____

_____

_____

_____

_____

To be clear, Peter is specifically addressing wives and husbands in these verses. He presents specific behaviors and characteristics that would turn an unbelieving husband to the Lord. How can these principles be applied to wise womanhood in a context outside of marriage? Make a list of these behaviors or characteristics that would influence or encourage others to obey God and live out their God-given purpose. Place a star beside anything you see modeled in Deborah.

_____

_____

_____

_____

_____

_____

_____

In Judges 5:12, Deborah and Barak sang to each other. Their musical harmony is evidence of their relational harmony. *They were not in competition with each other.*

What action word was sung to Deborah in Judges 5:12? _____

What action word was sung to Barak in Judges 5:12? _____

What picture does the word "arise" bring to mind for you? Write about it or draw it below.

Deborah could have sung, "Do something!" or "Step up!" or even "Why won't you lead?!" Instead, "Arise" was an invitation to step into God's plan. **The legacy of Deborah's life is that through her encouragement and influence, those whom God appointed to lead His people came forward**

**and stepped up to the plate to accept responsibility.** Ultimately, what does Deborah's attitude toward Barak reveal about her trust in the Lord?

_____

_____

_____

_____

_____

Based on Deborah's example, what impact could it have if Christian women chose to honor and celebrate the unique design and roles of both men and women?

_____

_____

_____

_____

_____

As you wrap up today's study, pause and ask the Lord to show you: Do you generally encourage or undermine those in leadership? Do you affirm godly leaders or do you insist they lead the way you think they should? How can you appropriately support those God has appointed as leaders in your home, church, community, and nation?

_____

_____

_____

_____

_____

_____

# Day 4: *The Battle Belongs to the Lord*

*Read Judges 5:13–23.*

Living for Jesus can feel like a battle. We fight our flesh as we resist the urge to let our world define who we are. We fight cultural messages that seek to erase the differences between men and women and that celebrate living outside of God's design. Despite the challenges, the battle to live out God's truth is a worthy one.

Revisit the map on page 8. Locate Deborah's palm and draw a dotted line to the place by the Kishon River where the Israelite army defeated Sisera's army.

What strikes you about the distance between these two locations? Write down your observations.

_____

_____

_____

_____

_____

Deborah lived in the southern portion of the land, in relative peace, far from the Canaanite strongholds in the northern part of her country. Still, she was aware of the threat and ready and available when God called her to do something about it. We can draw parallels from Deborah's story for the spiritual battles each of us must fight.

*Read Ephesians 6:10–18 below.* Underline all descriptions of our ultimate enemy. Circle all descriptions of the weapons Scripture urges us to use in the fight.

> Finally, be strong in the Lord and in the strength of his might. Put on the whole armor of God, that you may be able to stand against the schemes of the devil. For we do not wrestle against flesh and blood, but against the rulers, against the authorities, against the cosmic powers over this present darkness, against the spiritual forces of evil in the heavenly places. Therefore take up the whole armor of God, that you may be able to withstand in the evil day, and having done all, to stand firm.

> Stand therefore, having fastened on the belt of truth, and having put on the breastplate of righteousness, and, as shoes for your feet, having put on the readiness given by the gospel of peace. In all circumstances take up the shield of faith, with which you can extinguish all the flaming darts of the evil one; and take the helmet of salvation, and the sword of the Spirit, which is the word of God, praying at all times in the Spirit, with all prayer and supplication. To that end, keep alert with all perseverance, making supplication for all the saints.

Consider the battle language used in Judges 5:19–21. These verses poetically describe the battle between God's people and their enemies. The phrase "from heaven the stars fought" (v. 20) is a poetic way of saying that God divinely intervened on behalf of His people. God used creation as a weapon in His hand to win the victory.

What natural events do you think are being described in Judges 5:4–5?

_____

_____

_____

_____

The Kishon River that we read about in this passage is normally a shallow stream and at times a dry riverbed. The fact that Sisera was willing to take his chariots of iron into the river indicates that it was the dry season.

In God's providence, the chariots that the Canaanites thought were their strength became their liability. God sent a torrential downpour from heaven. The river overflowed and the Canaanite chariots became stuck in the mud.

What happened next according to Judges 5:21?

_____

_____

_____

_____

Were there bigger, spiritual implications for Israel's battle against the Canaanites? Write down whatever comes to mind.

_____

_____

_____

_____

_____

_____

Baal was the god of the Canaanites. He was considered the god of wars and storms. God demonstrated to the Canaanites and the Israelites, and to all who read the story of this battle, that He is the God of storms and wars, not Baal. He is the mighty conqueror.

*Review Judges 4:15–16 below.* Circle words that indicate who was responsible for Israel's victory.

> And the LORD routed Sisera and all his chariots and all his army before Barak by the edge of the sword. And Sisera got down from his chariot and fled away on foot. And Barak pursued the chariots and the army to Harosheth-hagoyim, and all the army of Sisera fell by the edge of the sword; not a man was left.

Who is the champion in this story? It's not Deborah. It's not Barak. Who routed Sisera and his chariots? God did. Who subdued Jabin the king of Canaan before the people of Israel? The Lord did.

God turned a dry riverbed into a raging torrent. Barak didn't do that. Deborah didn't do that. God did. The Israelites couldn't look back at this battle and claim responsibility for the victory. They stood on foot and watched as God intervened and they participated in what God did from heaven.

The Israelites could not win this victory on their own. They had been defeated for twenty years. The Canaanite army was well armed and battle ready. Humanly speaking, God's people had no hope of winning against this enemy, but God did it. God is the victor; God is the champion.

Write out Psalm 20:7 below.

_____

_____

_____

How does this verse remind you of Deborah's story? Explain.

_____

_____

_____

_____

Sisera and his army trusted in their military might, including their force of 900 chariots of iron (Judg. 4:3), but Deborah put her trust in the Lord. When we rely on our own human resources, abilities, efforts, strength, ingenuity, or strategies, we will discover that we are not strong enough to win the battle. To be women of influence, women who stand for God's truth and fight for God's people as Deborah did, our lives must declare, "we trust in the name of the Lord our God."

Deborah's story is a reminder that there is no limit to God's power. He can win any battle, any war, any victory over any person, any circumstance, any situation. He is able to conquer the hardest of hearts. If He wants to use the stars from heaven to fight, He will do that. If He wants to use a torrential downpour, He can. God is able to accomplish His purposes in our world and to overcome those who oppose Him and His people.

To wrap up today's study, write out Psalm 20 in your own words. This is a battle psalm that repeats the theme we find in Deborah's story—*every battle ultimately belongs to the Lord.*

_____

_____

_____

_____

_____

# Day 5: *Take It Home; Make It Personal*

*Read Genesis 1–3.*

Gender, gender roles, manhood, womanhood . . . these areas have become a battlefield in our culture. Where are you seeing the evidence of this battle?

_____

_____

_____

_____

You might think that the fight for biblically defined womanhood hasn't affected you directly, but the battle for truth comes to all of our lives, straight through our front door and into our hearts.

Take a moment to reflect using the prompts below.

GOD'S WAY SEEMS UNDER ATTACK IN THE AREA OF . . .

IT SOMETIMES FEELS LIKE THE ENEMY
IS WINNING IN THE AREA OF . . .

IN MY OWN LIFE, THE SPIRITUAL BATTLE
FEELS MOST INTENSE IN THE AREA OF . . .

Let's move from the Palm of Deborah to another tree, the tree of the knowledge of good and evil recorded in Genesis 1–3. In these first few chapters of Scripture we see the Four D cycle play out for the first time. God told Adam and Eve not to eat the fruit from the tree of the knowledge of good and evil (Gen. 2:17). They disobeyed and experienced divine discipline.

*Read the curse God gave to Adam and Eve as recorded in Genesis 3:16–19.*

How do you make sense of what God is saying in verse 16?

_____

_____

_____

_____

One of the consequences of the Fall is that men and women (particularly in the context of marriage) become competitive and controlling rather than honoring one another and working together for the good of each other and for the fulfillment of His purposes in our world. This often leads to jealousy, division, and discord.

How have you seen this in your own life?

_____

_____

_____

_____

Both men and women need the Spirit's help to redeem us from our sinful tendency to resent, resist, or rebel against God's design. Deborah's example shows us that it is possible to have influence without being demanding or manipulative and that our trust in God's will shows up in the ways we interact with others. Deborah was a part of God's plan as a prophetess and a judge, and she acted in ways that honored and built up the men around her without compromising God's design. Deborah's story reminds us of both the cultural battle for truth and the war that often rages inside our hearts. Though it may feel counterintuitive, **the battle is won through surrender to the Lord.**

Match the references below with corresponding verses about surrendering to God.

JAMES 4:7                          "He must increase, but I must decrease."

MATTHEW 16:24                      Submit yourselves therefore to God. Resist
                                   the devil, and he will flee from you.

JAMES 4:10                         Then Jesus told his disciples, "If anyone
                                   would come after me, let him deny himself
                                   and take up his cross and follow me."

JOHN 3:30                          "For whoever would save his life will lose
                                   it, but whoever loses his life for my sake
                                   will find it."

MATTHEW 16:25                      Humble yourselves before the Lord, and
                                   he will exalt you.

What does surrendering to God look like in your everyday life?

_____

_____

_____

_____

Use your imagination. Picture God raising up an army of "Deborahs," women willing to stand up for His truth. Picture a movement of true women of God: women who will radiate the life of Jesus in our world and use the "weapons" of faith and purity against opponents of God's Word. What difference could those women make in the world?

_____

_____

_____

_____

Pause and pray that God would raise up such a movement of women in our day—for His glory. Write out your prayer below.

_____

_____

_____

Is there an area of your life where you feel defeated? Like you are up against an impossible enemy? Reflect about that in the space below and ask the Lord to help you trust in His strength, not your own.

_____

_____

_____

_____

_____

_____

Spend time meditating on and memorizing the following verse this week:

THAT ALL THIS ASSEMBLY MAY KNOW THAT the Lord SAVES not with SWORD and SPEAR. for the BATTLE IS THE LORD'S, & He will give you into OUR HANDS.

1 SAMUEL 17:47

# Week 6

## Big Idea: YOU CAN IMPACT THE NEXT GENERATION FOR CHRIST.

Can discouragement lose a war?

It almost did in 1900 during the Boer War in South Africa. In a critical maneuver, Boer troops surrounded the town of Ladysmith. During the 118-day siege, tensions were high. *The survival of the whole town was at stake.*

During the siege, there was a civilian who would go in and out among the troops and make discouraging comments. He never fired a shot for the enemy; his words became bullets as he targeted the troops with his hostility.

The naysayer was eventually court-martialled and ultimately sentenced to a year in prison. The judge ruled that it was a crime to speak discouraging words during such desperate times.

Following God's calling on your life can feel like a battle. We all know what it's like to want to go AWOL (absent without leave). Deborah's story is a reminder though that God never promised us faith without a fight. He has promised to go with us into the battle.

## Day 1: *Good Soldiers*

*Read 2 Timothy 2:1–13.*

Did you ever sing this song as a child (or with your own children)?

*I may never march in the infantry.*
*Ride in the cavalry.*
*Shoot the artillery.*
*I may never fly o'er the enemy.*
*But I'm in the Lord's army.*

*Yes, sir!*

This picture of God's people being an army, ready to fight comes straight from Scripture. How does Paul describe Christ's followers in 2 Timothy 2:3?

_____

_____

_____

_____

What battle do you think this verse is referring to?

_____

_____

_____

_____

The fight Scripture calls us to is not a fight against culture or against each other but the fight for truth. We are to be "good soldiers," ready to keep fighting the war against sin and Satan's influence in our lives, our homes, our churches, and our communities.

As we continue looking at Deborah's story, we see examples to emulate and to avoid.

Three women are specifically described in Judges 4–5: Deborah, Jael, and Sisera's mother. Compare and contrast these three women using the chart below. What similarities do you see? What differences?

| DEBORAH | JAEL | SISERA'S MOTHER |
|---|---|---|
| Judges 4:4–14 | Judges 4:17–22, 5:24–27 | Judges 5:28–30 |

Both Deborah and Jael were ready to respond to God's call when it came. They were doing ordinary things, Deborah as a wife, mother, and judge, and Jael caring for her home, when God brought the battle to them. Both women chose to engage on behalf of God's people and for God's glory. What are some alternate ways they could have chosen to respond? Make a list.

_____

_____

_____

_____

_____

_____

Contrast Deborah and Jael's response with the response of Sisera's mother. Though her name isn't listed in Scripture, what does Judges 5:28 tell us she was doing as the battle raged?

_____

_____

What does verse 30 reveal about what she hoped the outcome of the battle would be?

_____

_____

Rather than serving the Lord through everyday faithfulness, Sisera's mother holed up and fretted, revealing that her hope was in the battle's outcome, not in the Lord. Instead of longing to see God glorified, she longed to see the Canaanites pillage the people of God. Deborah and Jael did not initiate the battle, but when the fighting came to them, they were ready and chose to fight on the Lord's side. Like these three women, our willingness to serve God daily and our readiness to engage as the Lord leads reveals something about our hearts and our trust in Him.

Look up the following verses. Next to each reference write ways you can live a life of everyday faithfulness, ready to be used as the Lord sees fit.

PSALM 100:4-5

PSALM 119:11

PROVERBS 3:3-4

ROMANS 12:12

EPHESIANS 4:32

*Revisit the armor of God described in Ephesians 6:10–20.* What are some practical ways you can take up the armor described in these verses?

_____

_____

_____

_____

_____

_____

_____

_____

_____

An enemy army may not invade your nation's borders as it did for Deborah. A war general may not come to your front door like one did for Jael. What kinds of "battles" are more likely to come into your world?

_____

_____

_____

_____

Are you ready and willing to join the battle as the Lord leads? Or are you more prone to hide? Take time to reflect.

_____

_____

_____

_____

_____

As you put yourself at God's disposal, as you become a willing instrument in His cause, He will move heaven and earth if necessary to defend you and to glorify Himself. Deborah's story can encourage you that when you get into a circumstance that seems impossible, you don't have to fight the battle on your own. There are times when He calls us to rise up and be a part of the army of faith. We can armor up and be ready, knowing that God will do whatever He has to do to glorify Himself and fulfill His purposes in our lives and in our world.

Wrap up today's study by meditating on 2 Timothy 4:7–8. Consider: do these words encourage any specific response from you?

> I have fought the good fight, I have finished the race, I have kept the faith. Henceforth there is laid up for me the crown of righteousness, which the Lord, the righteous judge, will award to me on that day, and not only to me but also to all who have loved his appearing.

# Day 2: *Don't Go AWOL*

*Read Judges 5:2–23.*

As Deborah and Barak retold the story of the fight with Canaan through their victory song, they pointed out that some were more willing to get involved than others. Skim through these verses once again. Make a list of those who willingly came to Barak and Deborah's aid and those who sat out of the battle.

| WILLING TO FIGHT | SAT IT OUT |
|---|---|
|  |  |

Several of the tribes of Israel are named as willing participants in the battle: Ephraim, Benjamin, Manasseh, Zebulun, Issachar, and Naphtali. *Compare this list with Judges 1:27–34.* What changes do you see in the people of these tribes during Deborah's day?

_____

_____

_____

_____

_____

_____

_____

Surely, the men of these tribes were scared. The Canaanites were an intimidating enemy! But these Israelites followed God; they followed their leaders. They got involved. They risked their lives and went into the battle.

Naphtali and Zebulun were the tribes most directly affected by the problem. They lived where the Canaanite powers had been centered. They lived closest to King Jabin, and as a result likely experienced the greatest oppression from the enemy. It's not surprising they got involved. They had a lot to gain and a lot to lose.

There were others who lived nearby but refused to get involved. How does Judges 5:15–16 describe the tribe of Reuben?

_____

_____

_____

_____

_____

They had "great searchings of heart." They contemplated getting involved, but when it came down to it, they stayed among the sheepfolds where it was safe. Where there wasn't a threat. They chose to let their brethren go to war without their aid. Three other tribes chose not to fight and are listed in Judges 5:17. List them below.

_____

_____

_____

These four tribes stayed home to attend to their own business. There's nothing wrong with that in times of peace, but there are times when we are called to go into battle, times when we must get involved in ways that involve risk. These four tribes were unwilling to do that. As a result, they were exposed by Barak and Deborah for their inactivity.

*Record Jesus' words found in Matthew 12:30 and Luke 11:23.*

_____

_____

_____

_____

_____

_____

What do you think Jesus meant?

_____

_____

_____

_____

It may sound severe, but Scripture indicates that to sit back and do nothing when God asks for your help is actually to become His enemy. We can't stay neutral in the battle for God's truth.

Look up the following passages. Next to each one, list what Scripture calls us to fight for.

PSALM 41:1

PROVERBS 31:8-9

ISAIAH 56:1

MATTHEW 28:18-20

PHILIPPIANS 1:18

1 TIMOTHY 6:12

JAMES 4:7

God didn't need the absent tribes in order to win the victory against Sisera's army. God did it without their help. This story is a reminder that God will win the victory over evil in this world. His kingdom will come and His will will be done on earth as it is in heaven.

But if we go AWOL and choose to tend strictly to our own business when God has called us to cry out through prayer and to wage spiritual warfare on behalf of the Church and others, *we miss an incredible opportunity to align ourselves with God.* **Often, it is the fear of trouble, the love of ease, and an inordinate affection for our worldly business that keeps us out of the battle.**

If we do not get involved as God directs, we will face disgrace for sitting out of the battle. But those who are willing to lay down our lives, to willingly get involved at the Lord's commission and His calling will experience the joy of having participated with God in the battle.

You can pick up the sword of truth and join the battle any time from anywhere. Start now. Wrap up today's study by interceding for God's Church to be a force that pushes back the darkness.

## Day 3: *Encouragement, Our Secret Weapon*

*Read Hebrews 10:19–25.*

What weapon did Deborah bring to war? She wasn't a soldier. She was a wife and a mother. *One of the weapons Deborah used was encouragement.*

Deborah inspired Barak to do what God called him to do and to be who God called him to be. Through her words of encouragement, she deployed an army.

Who has encouraged you in your walk with Christ? What does he or she do or say that is so encouraging?

_____

_____

_____

_____

_____

*Revisit Hebrews 10:19–25 below.* Underline reasons this passage gives us to have confidence in the Lord. Circle the actions this passage calls us to as a result of our confidence in Him.

> Therefore, brothers, since we have confidence to enter the holy places by the blood of Jesus, by the new and living way that he opened for us through the curtain, that is, through his flesh, and since we have a great priest over the house of God, let us draw near with a true heart in full assurance of faith, with our hearts sprinkled clean from an evil conscience and our bodies washed with pure water. Let us hold fast the confession of our hope without wavering, for he who promised is faithful. And let us consider how to stir up one another to love and good works, not neglecting to meet together, as is the habit of some, but encouraging one another, and all the more as you see the Day drawing near.

Deborah's encouragement was an outflow of her trust in the Lord. When we trust the Lord and when we are committed to living according to His Word, encouragement will naturally flow out of us and strengthen others.

Practically, how can we "stir up one another to love"?

_____

_____

_____

_____

_____

_____

_____

_____

Encouragement is more than a happy thought or warm sentiment. True, biblical encouragement is the habit of reminding the people of God of the promises of God, just like Deborah did. We can follow Deborah's example as women of influence through God-exalting encouragement.

*Read Colossians 3:16–17.*

When we are Word-filled women (letting the Word dwell in us richly) it spills out of our hearts and mouths and encourages others who are seeking to live for Christ. Think of letting God's Word dwell in you like the hub of the wheel. What are the "spokes" or the ways that will radiate out according to this passage?

The *Word* in me

The book of Judges is not ultimately about Deborah and Barak. It's not about a single victory. It is a book about God's people living *together*. It is the story of the *nation* of Israel rebelling against God and experiencing the redemption of God. In the same way, your story is not just about you. You are a part of the family of God and you can have a profound effect on others through your encouragement.

Imagine the impact if God would raise up in our day not just one woman but thousands of women around the world, women who will arise like Deborah did, women with clarity, courage, conviction, faith, and humility. Women who are willing to say, "Yes, Lord." Women whose lives will inspire the men and women around them to believe God for what only He can do. Describe what that would be like.

_____

_____

_____

_____

_____

_____

_____

Who are some women you know who want to live for Christ, who want to live out His good design for their womanhood, and who want to stand for truth? Make a list of the names that come to mind.

_____

_____

_____

_____

_____

_____

_____

To wrap up today's study, pray and ask the Lord to give you promises from His Word to encourage these individuals. Write those promises next to the names on your list and then look for ways to strengthen others through encouragement.

# Day 4: *From Generation to Generation*

*Read Psalm 145.*

Write out the passages listed below. Draw an arrow connecting the two.

JUDGES 4:23                                    JUDGES 5:31

Notice the order of events. **First the battle, then the rest.** This is the same order of events in our lives. Women of influence know they cannot bypass the fight for truth. There is no fast track to peace.

The spiritual battle in our day is no less intense than it was in Deborah's day, and the enemy is no less powerful. God is chastening His people for our sins and idolatry, as He did in Deborah's generation. As in Deborah's day, there is a need for women to stand on the promises of God and to speak God's Word faithfully, even when it is challenging.

How many years did Israel experience peace after Jabin and Sisera were defeated (Judg. 5:31)?

_____

Remember: how many years did the Israelites experience the oppression of King Jabin (Judg. 4:3)?

_____

In His mercy, God allowed His people to experience peace and freedom for twice as long as they were oppressed. What changes do you think Deborah saw during those forty years of peace? Make a list.

_____

_____

_____

_____

_____

The impact of Deborah's life: her courage, her faith, her godly influence, was felt not only in her generation but in the next. Her willingness to obey God and to stand on His truth was a blessing to her generation and the generations that followed. Her story prompts us to wrestle with the question: what mark will our lives have on this generation and on those who are coming behind us?

Psalm 145 tells us that "one generation shall commend your works to another" (v. 4). God's people are called to be intentional about leaving a legacy. Make a list of the character traits of God listed in Psalm 145. Place a star beside every truth that was exemplified in Deborah's life.

_____

_____

_____

_____

_____

How would you summarize Deborah's legacy? Write about it in a sentence or two below.

_____

_____

_____

Yes, Deborah made an impact as a woman of influence, willing to go to war against an enemy of God's people. But she also served God faithfully day after day, year after year in her God-given assignment as a wife, mother, and wise judge. God used her faithfulness and courage to usher in peace for an entire generation.

Consider the roles God has assigned to your life. Where has God asked you to demonstrate everyday faithfulness to the next generation?

_____

_____

_____

_____

_____

What battles has God asked you to fight in His name?

_____

_____

_____

_____

_Read Deuteronomy 6:5–7._ What are the practical ways these verses encourage us to pass the baton of truth to the next generation?

_____

_____

_____

To wrap up today's study, prayerfully consider your own legacy. What do you want to commend from one generation to the next? Make a list.

_____

_____

_____

_____

_____

_____

# Day 5: *Take It Home; Make It Personal*

*Read Judges 4–5 once more.*

Use the reflection questions that follow to consider what you've learned through this study.

What does Deborah's story reveal about God?

_____

_____

_____

What inspires you about Deborah's story?

_____

_____

_____

What challenges you about Deborah's story?

_____

_____

_____

Are there any questions that linger in your mind about this text?

_____

_____

_____

_____

What does it mean to be a woman of influence?

_____

_____

_____

_____

Where can you turn when you feel weary from the battle for God's truth?

_____

_____

_____

_____

In what areas of your life do you feel oppressed by the enemy right now?

_____

_____

_____

_____

What truths from God's Word give you courage?

_____

_____

_____

_____

Wrap up this study by writing out a prayer, asking God to help you be a woman of godly influence on those around you. Adapt the prayer below or write your own.

Lord, I am weak, but You are strong. O Lord, I am small, but You are great. I am sinful, but You are holy. I am afraid at times, but You are the God who gives faith—not in myself, through my own strength or efforts but in the great arms of Jehovah God, the God of the storms, the God of heaven and earth.

Lord, I pray for my Christian sisters around the world and for myself, that You would grant us all that is needed in this season to say "yes" to You and "no" to our flesh. Help us to press into the battle. Help us Lord. Give us courage. In Your name I pray. Amen.

———————

# Week 1:

- While the rebellion of the Israelites seems obvious to us, we can easily become stubborn and fall into the same cycle of disobedience. How have you seen patterns of sin reflected in your own life?

- We are always worshiping something. What are some steps you can take to keep God as the center of your attention and focus of your worship?

- As you examine the actions of the Israelites and the cycle of the Four Ds (Disobedience, Discipline, Desperation, Deliverance), what do you see about God's character?

- How have you seen God's loving discipline in your life lead to something good? Did you consider His discipline a gift at the time?

- What specific way(s) might God be wanting to use you as an instrument in someone's life?

# Week 2:

- As believers, we are all called to reflect the image of God. What specific roles has He given you in this season? Consider how you can demonstrate His character and love in those places.

- Think about the mothers/mother-like figures God has placed in your life. Describe the impact they have made and how the Lord has worked through them.

- How are you personally encouraged by Deborah's example as a woman of influence?

- What are you allowing to shape your identity? Are you finding your security in God's Word and His design?

- Describe the differences between the cultural view of womanhood and the biblical perspective. How do you want to see the Lord grow you as a godly woman?

---

## Week 3:

- When God asks you to obey Him, what is your first response? In what kinds of situations do you find yourself most reluctant to obey?
- Gideon did not feel qualified for the job God gave him. What hesitations keep you from embracing God's call on your life?
- Our natural tendency is to rely on our strengths. Why do you think God chooses to use our weaknesses for His purposes? How has God given you a different perspective on your weaknesses?
- The responsibilities given to Deborah, Barak, Gideon, and Jael were all different but equally important in terms of carrying out what the Lord called them to do. What opportunities has God placed before you to be faithful in, whether big or small?
- How can you share the gospel today through your words and actions? Take some time to pray and ask how the Lord would use you to share His hope with someone.

## Week 4:

- Where did Deborah's confidence come from? Do you find yourself placing your confidence in this world or in the Word of God?
- Why is it so important to study and know Scripture? What are the benefits of having God's Word implanted in your heart?
- When was the last time God spoke to you through His Word? Describe what you learned, or ask Him what He wants to teach you.
- Who do you know who is a wise, Word-filled woman, like Deborah? What are some of her characteristics you want to be evident in your life?
- What is one of your favorite promises of God? Ask the Lord to embed that truth in your heart and grow you into a Word-filled woman.

 Listen in as women discuss this study in the *Women of the Bible* podcast by *Revive Our Hearts*. Find it at ReviveOurHearts.com/Deborah.

# Week 5

- How does the world push back against God's design for womanhood? How can you stand firm in your God-given identity and encourage others to do the same?
- What similarities do you see between the culture Deborah lived in and the one we live in today?
- How has Deborah's example inspired you to embrace God's plan for womanhood? What characteristics of Deborah do you admire the most?
- How can you come alongside the men in your life and encourage them in the role the Lord has given them?
- Do you find it difficult to trust God for your identity? What battles most frequently rage in your heart?

# Week 6

- When God calls you to action, is your immediate response, "Yes, Lord" or do you hesitate? Is there a step God is asking you to take right now?
- How can you use encouragement as a weapon, like Deborah? Think of one specific way you can encourage someone today.
- Deborah's choice to obey the Lord had a lasting effect for generations. What do you hope others will say about the way you lived your life?
- Why do our small acts of faithfulness matter? How can you remind yourself that God is working, even when your actions seem insignificant?
- As you've studied Deborah's life, what truths have you learned about the Lord? What familiar truths have been renewed in your heart as a result of this study?

# Notes

## Week 1: From Disobedience to Deliverance

1 "Intro to Judges," The NIV Study Bible (The International Bible Society), accessed April 30, 2021, https://www.biblica.com/resources/scholar-notes/niv-study-bible/intro-to-judges/.

2 True Woman conferences are hosted by *Revive Our Hearts* to help women around the world experience personal revival.

3 "Instrument," Dictionary.com (Dictionary.com), accessed February 4, 2020, https://www.dictionary.com/browse/instrument?s=t).

## Week 2: The Power of Valor

1 "Differences Between Men and Women," Relationship Institute, April 12, 2021, https://relationship-institute.com/differences-between-men-and-women/.

2 This day's study is adapted from *True Woman 101 Divine Design: an Eight-Week Study on Biblical Womanhood* by Mary A. Kassian and Nancy DeMoss Wolgemuth (Chicago, IL: Moody Publishers, 2012), 68–71. Used by permission.

3 Elisabeth Elliot, *Let Me Be a Woman* (Carol Stream, IL: Tyndale House Publishers, 1976), 61.

4 Matthew Henry, "Proverbs 31 Bible Commentary," Proverbs 31 Bible Commentary - Matthew Henry (complete), accessed May 9, 2021, https://www.christianity.com/bible/commentary.php?com=mh&b=20&c=31.

5 "Valor," Merriam-Webster (Merriam-Webster), accessed May 9, 2021, https://www.merriam-webster.com/dictionary/valor.

# Notes

## Week 3: Unexpected Warriors

[1] As told to Erin Davis, Roland's granddaughter.

[2] Charles Spurgeon, "Faith's Checkbook, by C. H. Spurgeon," accessed May 11, 2021, https://archive.spurgeon.org/fcb/fcb-bod.htm.

## Week 4: The Power of a Word-Filled Woman

[1] David Guzik, "The Greatness and Glory of God's Word: Study Guide for Psalm 119," Blue Letter Bible, accessed May 14, 2021, https://www.blueletterbible.org/Comm/guzik_david/StudyGuide2017-Psa/Psa-119.cfm.

[2] C. Samuel Storms, More Precious than Gold: 50 Daily Meditations on the Psalms (Wheaton, IL: Crossway Books, 2009), 213.

[3] Nancy Leigh DeMoss, A Place of Quiet Rest: Finding Intimacy with God through a Devotional Life (Chicago, IL: Moody Publishers, 2000), 146–147. Used by permission.

## Week 5: A True Women's Movement

[1] John Angell James, Female Piety: The Young Woman's Friend and Guide through Life to Immortality (Morgan, PA: Soli Deo Gloria, 1995), 72.

[2] Ibid.

# Reflections

# Reflections

# Reflections

# Reflections